Also by Bruce Pandolfini:

CHESS TARGET PRACTICE
MORE CHESS OPENINGS: TRAPS AND ZAPS 2
BEGINNING CHESS
PANDOLFINI'S CHESS COMPLETE
CHESSERCIZES
MORE CHESSERCIZES
CHECKMATE
LET'S PLAY CHESS
BOBBY FISCHER'S OUTRAGEOUS CHESS MOVES
ONE-MOVE CHESS BY THE CHAMPIONS
PRINCIPLES OF THE NEW CHESS
THE ABC'S OF CHESS
KASPAROV'S WINNING CHESS TACTICS
RUSSIAN CHESS
THE BEST OF CHESS LIFE AND REVIEW, Volume 1
THE BEST OF CHESS LIFE AND REVIEW, Volume 2
PANDOLFINI'S ENDGAME COURSE
CHESS OPENINGS: TRAPS AND ZAPS

SQUARE

The Best Chess Drill Book

ONE

for Beginners of All Ages

BRUCE PANDOLFINI

A FIRESIDE BOOK

Published by Simon & Schuster Inc.
New York   London   Toronto   Sydney   Tokyo   Singapore

FIRESIDE
Rockefeller Center
1230 Avenue of the Americas
New York, New York 10020

FIRESIDE and colophon are registered trademarks
of Simon & Schuster Inc.

Designed by Irving Perkins Associates
Manufactured in the United States of America

10 9 8 7 6 5 4 3 2

Library of Congress Catologing-in-Publication Data

Pandolfini, Bruce.
    Square one : the best chess drill book for beginners of all ages /
Bruce Pandolfini.
        p.   cm.
    "A Fireside book."
    Includes index.
    1. Chess.   2. Chess problems.   I. Title.
    [GV1446.P344   1994]
    794.1'2—dc20   94-17956
                                                    CIP

ISBN: 0-671-88424-7

This one is for Jimmy

Acknowledgments

I would like to thank Carol Ann Caronia especially, who helped devise the concept, format, and overall presentation. Her contribution was invaluable. My gratitude also goes to Idelle Pandolfini, Deborah Bergman, Bruce Alberston, Renée Rabb, Burt Hochberg, Ted Johnson, Bonni Leon, and Larry Tamarkin. I also appreciate the valuable talents of my editor, Laura Yorke, who put the whole thing together.

Contents

Introduction

Are you a games-player? Does solving puzzles challenge you? If your answer is "yes" to these questions, then chess is your baby. You'll find it a truly satisfying pastime, one that has already attracted millions of fans around the world.

It's a game that's been around for a long time, but it always seems new and different. Nobody knows who invented chess, though it appears to have originated in the fifth century A.D. in the Indus Valley, between India and Persia. Eventually the game made its way around the globe, evolving and taking on character, with most of its rules finally becoming set about 400 years ago. Today, no matter where you are, you'll have no trouble making friends if chess is the common language.

I won't argue, as do some experts, that chess develops intelligence. But I will posit what countless educators have come to know: that playing chess provides practice for solving problems. And what is intelligence if it's not the ability to solve problems? Play the game and discover that the techniques used to analyze chess situations can also be used, sometimes quite creatively, to grapple with puzzling questions at work or in school.

Square One teaches the fundamentals in seven chapters, covering all the moves and rules, chess notation, checkmate and the game's essential principles. It also provides a cornucopia of examples to hone logic and critical thinking skills.

The book starts at the very beginning and explains everything step by step. Ranks and files, notation, moves of the pieces, the special rules of castling, promotion, and capturing *en passant* are clearly described. You will also learn how to win by attacking, checking, and checkmating.

Square One is a drill book. It lets you practice chess paradigms over and over until you really understand them. Its guiding theme is simple: Use an idea or solve a type of puzzle a few times and you master it. This is the active principle that the best way to learn anything, and certainly games, is by "doing." Working through the text is tantamount to contesting hundreds of real chess match-ups. Whether your goal is friendly play or serious competition, *Square One* should give you the confidence and foundation needed to succeed.

How to Use This Book

Square One is really two books in one. It's an introductory manual for beginners and a collection of tactical puzzles for experienced players. More than a hundred of the book's diagrams contain checkmates of one, two, or three moves. As you read, you are not told which diagrams conceal the mates and the beginner can ignore them. But if you wish, you can find these harder checkmate puzzles listed in the back of the book, pages 241–43. So you can read *Square One* at least twice—the first time as a beginner, learning moves and rules; the second time as a veteran player, solving checkmate puzzles.

If you are new to the game, start at the beginning. Read each explanation, looking at the diagram and answering the associated questions. If any of the material seems obvious, and you already feel comfortable with its content, just skip it. You can always go back for clarification. As for monitoring your progress, check answers (pages 179–240) as you go along, or after finishing a chapter.

After completing *Square One* the first time, peruse it again for reinforcement and to learn even more. Simply leaf through the checkmate puzzle section in the back (pages 241–43). See which diagrams offer one-move checkmates. Track them down and try to solve them. These answers are given on pages 244–46.

One-move checkmates are patently the easiest to solve. Just visualize the next move. A one-move checkmate for White means that White makes a move and mates. A one-move checkmate for Black means that Black moves and mates.

Don't stop there. After you've done all the one-movers, wrestle with the mates that take two moves. For each one, picture your first move, your opponent's reply, and your winning second move. As a final task, go back into the text to solve the three-movers. A three-move checkmate for White means that White plays and Black answers; White plays a second move and Black answers again; and White plays a third move giving checkmate.

This is a basic chess book with multi-level problems. It doesn't attempt to go where no player has gone before. It merely suggests that a good place to start is *Square One*.

SQUARE ONE

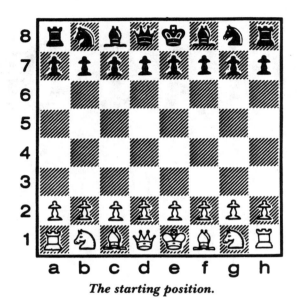

The starting position.

CHAPTER 1

The Chessboard and the Chessmen

This is a chessboard. It has alternating light and dark squares.

Most chessboards are black and white, but some are brown and white, and some are other colors, too. All chessboards have the same pattern of light and dark squares. Each chessboard has the same number of squares on it. Count the squares in Diagram 1 and see what you can learn about chessboards.

Diagram 1

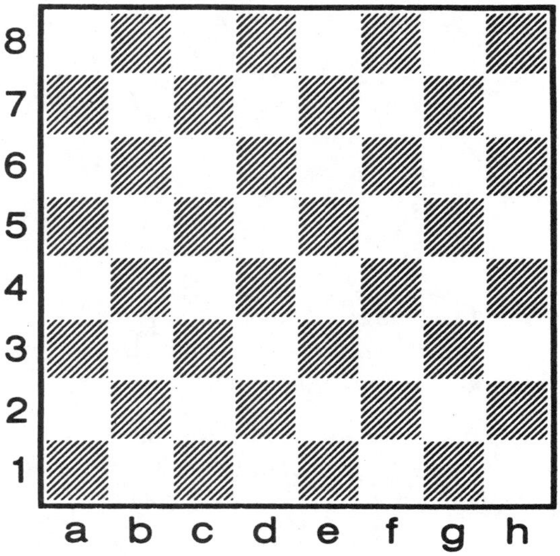

1. How many squares go across from left to right? _____

2. How many squares go from the bottom up? _____

3. How many squares are there altogether? _____

4. How many dark squares are there? _____

5. How many light squares are there? _____

Now check your answers against those given in Answers for Chapter 1, pages 179–85.

The letters a, b, c, d, e, f, g, and h are under the chessboard, going across from left to right. These letters are under rows of squares that go up and down the board. These rows are called *files. Files are lines of squares that go up and down the chessboard.*

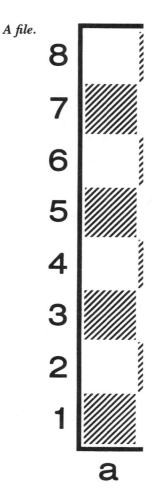

A file.

The numbers 1, 2, 3, 4, 5, 6, 7, and 8 are alongside the chessboard. These numbers are next to lines of squares going across the board. They are *ranks. Ranks are lines of squares that go across the chessboard.*

A rank.

Each square on the chessboard can be named by its file and its rank. Square a1 is in the file *a* and the rank *1*. We will sometimes be using this naming system in this chapter, and we will study it in more detail in Chapter 2.

Even though every chessboard is the same and has alternating light and dark squares on all sides, it makes a difference which way you turn the chessboard when you set up to play chess. When you set up a chessboard, each player should have a light square in the lower right corner facing him or her.

Remember the saying: **Light on the right!**

**A light square
on the right.**

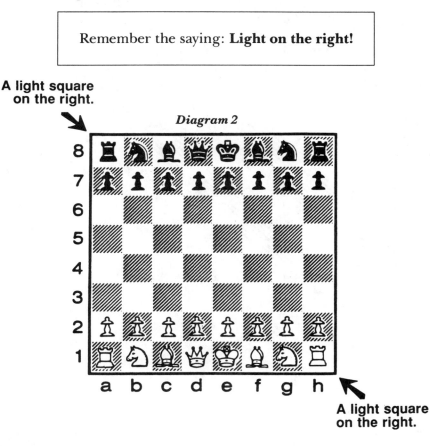

Diagram 2

**A light square
on the right.**

In this book, the White pieces always start at the bottom of the diagram and the Black pieces start at the top, as in Diagram 2.

Looking at the chessboard in Diagram 1, you can see slanted lines of squares of the same colors. These lines are *diagonals*.

6. Draw a line through the longest light
diagonal in Diagram 1. (Hint: It has
eight squares.)

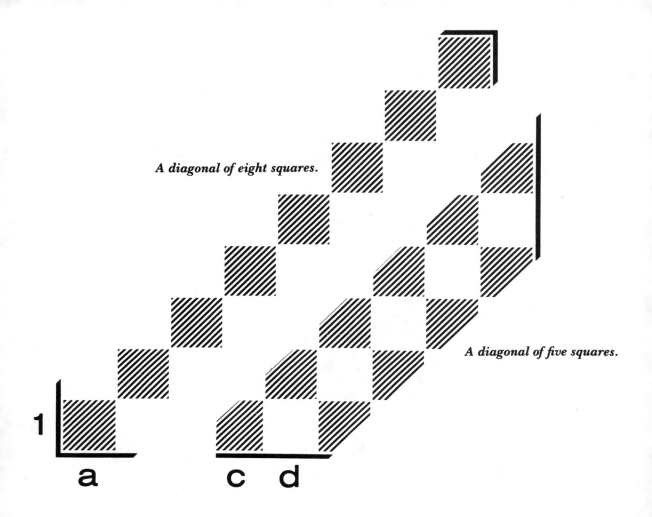

A diagonal of eight squares.

A diagonal of five squares.

1

a   c   d

7. In Diagram 1, circle one of the shortest
dark diagonals. (Hint: There are two of
these short, dark diagonals and they
have two squares each.)

Every chess set includes a White army and a Black one. The White
army has eight pieces and eight Pawns. The Black army also has
eight pieces and eight Pawns. Pawns and pieces are the chessmen or
men. They are always called White and Black, even though their
actual colors may be white and brown, yellow and red, or any two
light and dark colors.

The chessmen.

White		Black
♔	1 King	♚
♕	1 Queen	♛
♖ ♖	2 Rooks	♜ ♜
♗ ♗	2 Bishops	♝ ♝
♘ ♘	2 Knights	♞ ♞
♙ ♙ ♙ ♙ ♙ ♙ ♙ ♙	8 Pawns	♟ ♟ ♟ ♟ ♟ ♟ ♟ ♟

8. How many pieces are in the White and Black armies combined?

———————

9. How many Pawns are in the White and Black armies combined?

———————

10. How many men are in both armies combined? ——————————

Chessmen (pieces and Pawns) can do either of two things:

Chessmen can move to open squares, which means they can go from one square on the chessboard to another square.

Chessmen can capture enemy men, which means they take an enemy piece or Pawn off the board. The only piece that can't be captured is the King. When an enemy is taken, the chessman that captured it moves to the same square the enemy chessman used to sit on. The piece or Pawn that captures an enemy takes its place on the board. (Exception: Pawns sometimes capture other Pawns in a special way called *en passant,* as you will see.)

Pawns

This is a Pawn.

At the start of a chess game, White's Pawns sit on the 2nd rank and Black's Pawns sit on the 7th rank.

A Pawn can move straight ahead either one or two squares on its first move. After that, it can move only one square ahead at a time, even if it didn't go two squares on its first move.

Black's Pawns go

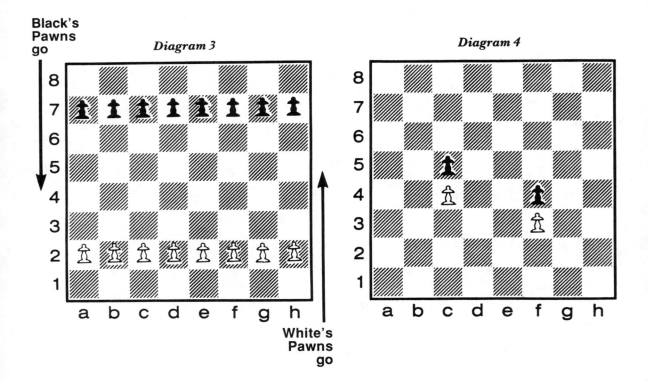

Diagram 3

Diagram 4

White's Pawns go

Pawns can never jump over other pieces or Pawns. If blocked, a Pawn cannot move straight ahead until the other piece or Pawn gets out of the way.

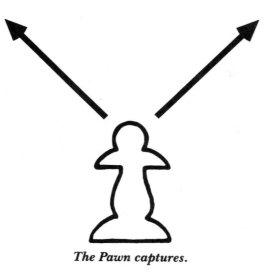

The Pawn captures.

11. In Diagram 5, mark the squares
where these Pawns could go on their
first moves.

Diagram 5

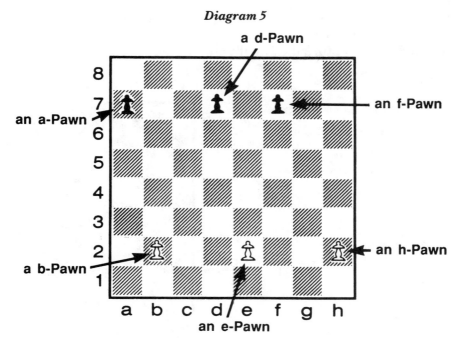

12. In Diagram 6, all the Pawns have had their first moves. Some have moved two squares and some only one square. Mark the squares where the Pawns could move on their second moves.

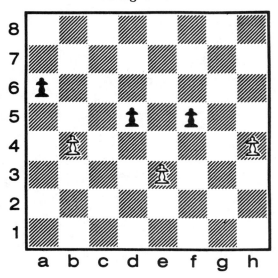

Diagram 6

Pawns can *never* move backward. Once advanced, they must stay advanced. This is one reason we should make our Pawn moves with care. If any other chessman is moved to a bad square, that same chessman sometimes can be played back to where it was after your opponent moves. Sometimes it can be moved to another square on the next turn. Pawns cannot do this. They can only go forward. They can never turn back.

Pawns can capture enemy pieces and Pawns. When a Pawn captures, it does so one square ahead *diagonally* to the left or right. The Pawn in Diagram 7 could capture the Knight on the left.

13. Draw a circle around the other piece in Diagram 7 that the Pawn could capture.

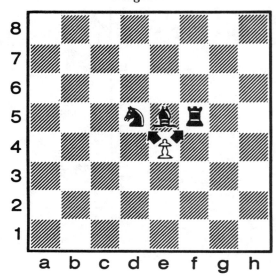

Diagram 7

Two special rules concerning Pawns are *en passant* capture and Queening.

When a Pawn Queens, it magically becomes whichever piece the player wants. Later in this book, in Chapter 6, we will learn more about Queening.

En passant is a French term meaning "in passing." In Diagram 8, the White Pawn sits on a square from which it can take the Black Pawn if the Black Pawn advances only one square on its first move. (The square on which the White Pawn is sitting is three squares forward from the square where it started the game.)

Black's Pawn has not been moved from its original square, so it can move either one square or two squares. You might think Black's Pawn could sneak past White's Pawn. But if Black's Pawn tries to avoid being captured by moving two squares ahead instead of only one, White can take it anyway. The *en passant* rule allows White's Pawn to capture Black's Pawn just as if Black's Pawn had moved only one square ahead. So whether Black's Pawn moves one or two squares ahead, it can be captured by White's Pawn on the same square.

Diagram 8

14. White wants to capture Black's Pawn. Can White take Black's Pawn if Black's Pawn advances two squares?

   _____

15. Will Black lose the Pawn if it doesn't advance at all? _____

16. Will White be able to capture Black's Pawn if Black's Pawn advances only one square? _____.

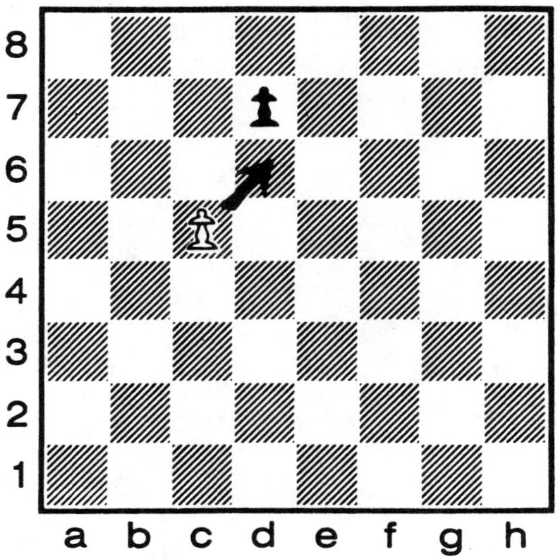

In Diagrams 9, 10, and 11, the White Pawn advances two squares and Black takes it *en passant*.

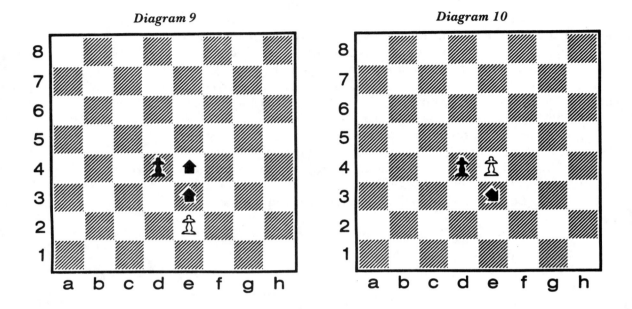

Diagram 9

Diagram 10

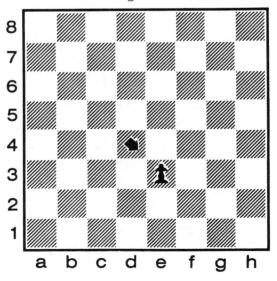

Diagram 11

Diagram 12

17. In Diagram 12, circle the Pawns
White can take if they advance two
squares.

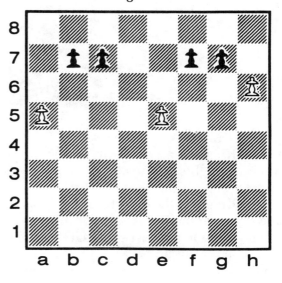

We have assigned each chess soldier a value, so that you may
understand how important each is compared to the others. There is
no chess rule that gives the soldiers number values, but thinking
about them in this way helps us to play better.

In our unofficial system,

The Pawn = 1.

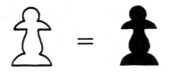

The value of a Pawn.

The Knight

This is a Knight.

The Knight is a *minor piece*. At the start of a chess game, each side has two Knights. White's Knights sit on b1 and g1. Black's Knights sit on b8 and g8.

The Knight is the *only* chess piece that can jump over other pieces and Pawns. It moves in the shape of an L, no matter what is in the way.

The Knight moves two squares in one direction and then one square at a right angle.

Or it can move one square in one direction and then two squares at a right angle.

Diagram 13

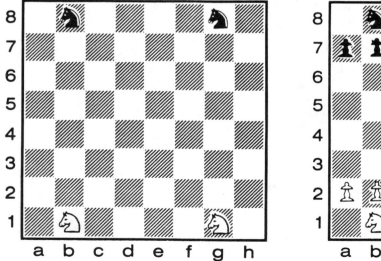

Diagram 14

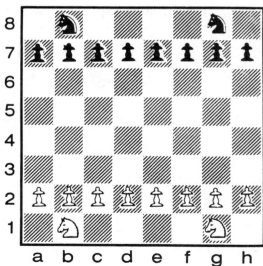

In Diagrams 15–1 and 15–2, the marked squares show that from the center a Knight may have as many as eight different moves.

A Knight can move forward or backward, to the left or right, but always in the shape of an L. It captures the enemy man sitting on the square on which it lands. (It cannot land on a square that is occupied by a friendly man.)

Diagram 15–1

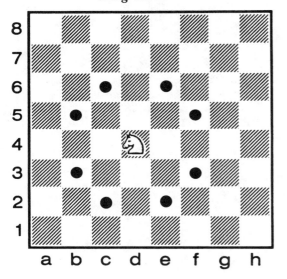

Diagram 15–2

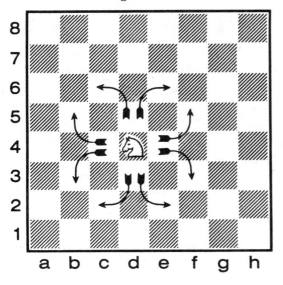

Diagram 16

18. In Diagram 16, we have crossed off a piece the Black Knight could capture. Which other pieces or Pawns could this Knight capture? Cross them off the diagram, too.

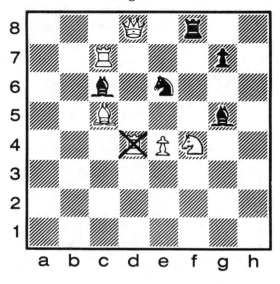

In our unofficial rating system, we have assigned the Knight a value, as we did for the Pawn. In this system,

The Knight = 3.

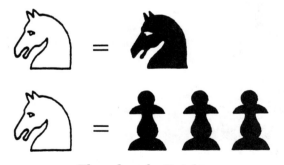

The value of a Knight.

The Bishop

This is a Bishop.

The Bishop is another *minor piece*. At the start of a chess game, each side has two Bishops, one on a dark square (c1 for White, f8 for Black) and one on a light square (f1 for White, c8 for Black).

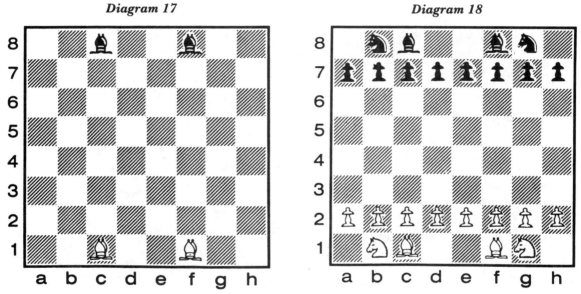

Diagram 17   *Diagram 18*

Bishops move along diagonals. They *cannot jump* over other pieces or Pawns.

Diagram 19

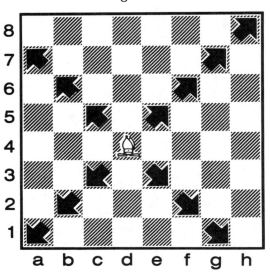

19. In Diagram 20, draw a line through the diagonal the Bishop can move along.

20. Which piece could it capture?

Diagram 20

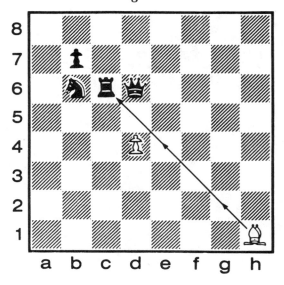

Bishops can capture the first enemy man that blocks their path on a diagonal.

If a Bishop starts out on a light square, it can *never* move to a dark square. If a Bishop starts out on a dark square, it can *never* move to a light square. Can the f1 Bishop move to f8? No!

Diagram 21

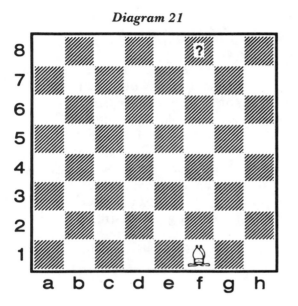

In our unofficial rating system, Bishops and Knights are worth about the same:

The Bishop = 3.

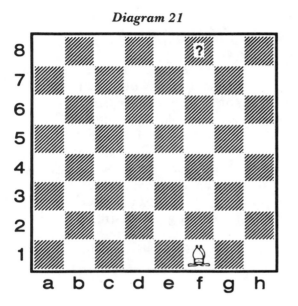

The value of a Bishop.

The Rook

This is the Rook.

The Rook is a *major piece*. You will soon see that Bishops and Knights are less valuable than Rooks and Queens. That is why we call Bishops and Knights *minor pieces* and Rooks and Queens *major pieces*.

At the start of a chess game, each side has two Rooks. They sit on the four corners of the chessboard, at a1 and h1 for White and a8 and h8 for Black.

A Rook can move straight along the rank it is on or straight along the file it is on, but it can only move in one direction at a time. A Rook cannot change directions on one turn. A Rook *cannot jump* over other pieces or Pawns, except in a special move called castling, which will be explained in Chapter 6.

Rooks can capture the first enemy man blocking their path by replacing it.

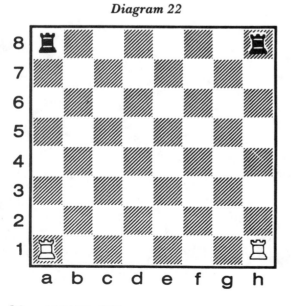

Diagram 22

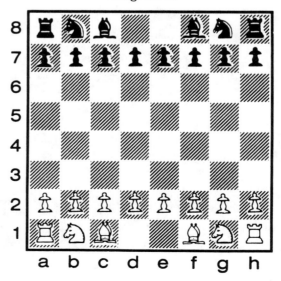

Diagram 23

21. In Diagram 24, draw a line straight through both of the two paths this Rook could follow.

22. Which men in Diagram 24 could the Rook take?

Diagram 24

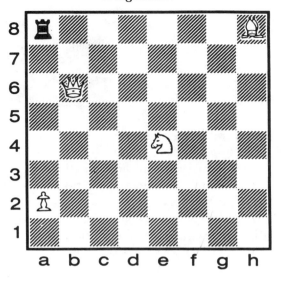

Rooks move *across dark and light squares alternately.* They can go forward and backward, to the left or to the right.

In our unofficial rating system, the Rook is more valuable than the Pawn, Knight, or Bishop:

The Rook = 5

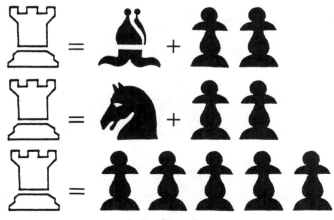

A Rook's value.

The Queen

This is the Queen.

The Queen is a *major piece*. At the start of a chess game, the Queen sits on d1 for White and d8 for Black. It always starts out *on the square of its own color*. That means a White Queen sits on a light square and a Black Queen sits on a dark square, as in Diagram 25.

The Queen is the most powerful piece on the chessboard. It can move like a Bishop. It can move like a Rook. It can move forward or backward, to the left or to the right. But the Queen cannot move like a Knight. It cannot jump over other pieces or Pawns.

Diagram 25

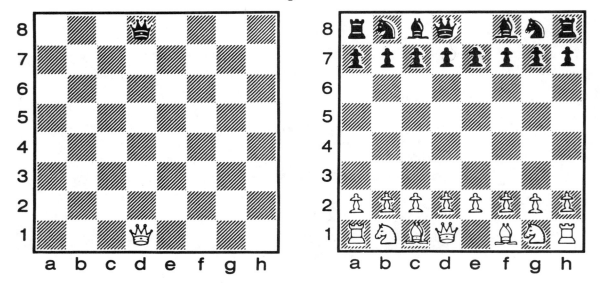

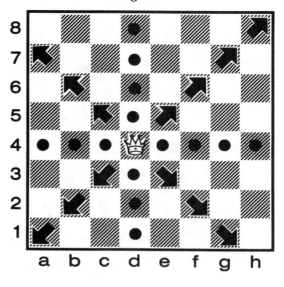

Diagram 26

23. In Diagram 26, the arrows and dots show all the possible paths the Queen on d4 might take. List all the squares on which the Queen can land. _____

_____

The Queen can capture the first enemy man blocking its path by replacing it on the board.

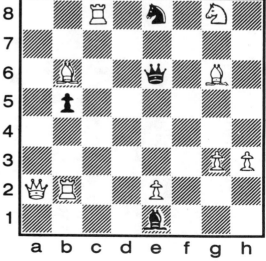

Diagram 27

24. Draw lines connecting the Black Queen and every piece or Pawn it could capture in Diagram 27. Check in the Answers for Chapter 1 section to see if you're right.

In our unofficial rating system, the Queen has the highest rating:

The Queen = 9

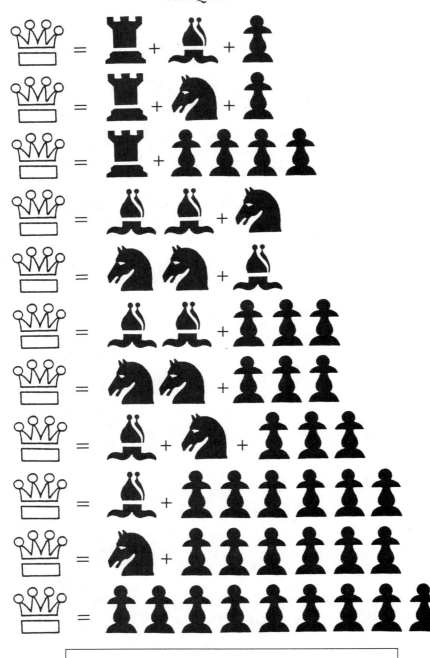

Remember: Bishops and Knights are minor pieces. Queens and Rooks are major pieces.

The King

This is the King. Without the King, the chess game is over.

The White King starts the chess game on e1, and the Black King starts on e8.

It is against the rules to move your King onto a square where it can be captured. If by accident you move your King to a square where it can be captured we say the move is *illegal*. Then the illegal move must be taken back, and another, legal move played.

Although the King is the most important piece on the chessboard, it is not as powerful as the Queen or Rook. The King can move in any direction, but only one square at a time.

Diagram 28

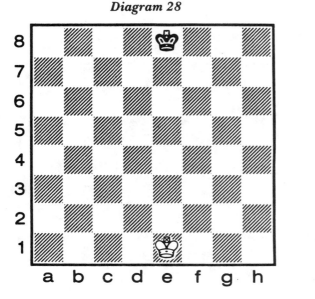

Diagram 29

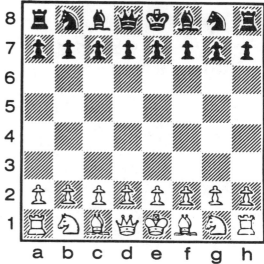

25. In Diagram 30, the squares to which the King could move are marked. List the names of the squares. _____

_____

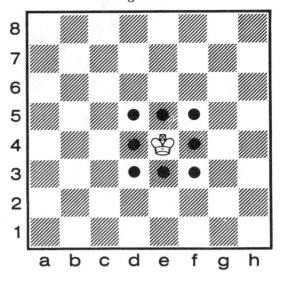

Diagram 30

The King can capture any unprotected enemy man on a square to which the King can move. But the King cannot capture a man that is protected by an enemy piece or Pawn, because if it did, the King would then be in a position where it could be captured itself. That would be an illegal move.

26. In Diagram 31, circle the pieces the King could capture.

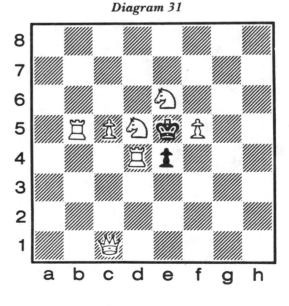

Diagram 31

Remember, there is one special rule about Kings. *They can never allow themselves to be captured.*

Enemy Kings can never get close enough to capture each other. There must *always* be at least one square between Kings. They can *never* get closer.

In Diagram 32, the King can move to any of the marked squares. Black's Rook protects the 'c-file and stops the King from moving there. If the King went to the c-file, it would be moving to a square where it could be captured, and that is illegal.

Diagram 32

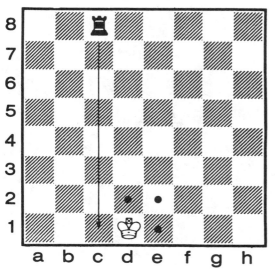

27. In Diagram 33, there is a Black King and a White King. Mark the squares to which they could move.

Diagram 33

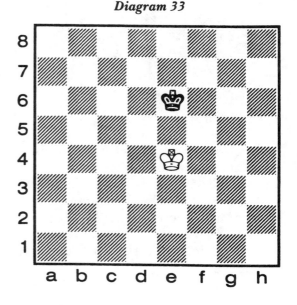

Since the King is not allowed to be captured, it is an infinitely valuable piece and cannot truly be given a numerical value.

Setting Up the Board

In Diagram 34, look at the way the pieces face each other across the chessboard. See that the same kinds of pieces oppose each other on the same files.

Black has a Rook on the a-file, and so does White. White has a Knight on the b-file, and so does Black. It is the same across the whole board.

Now that you know where all the pieces start, set up your chessboard to look exactly like Diagram 35.

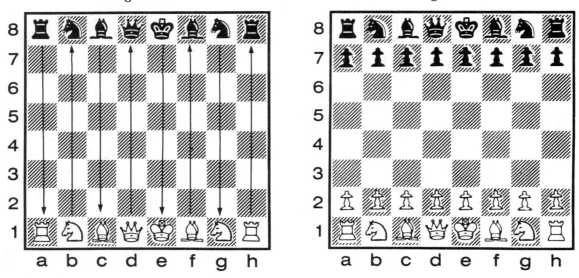

Diagram 34   *Diagram 35*

Offense and Defense

If you go first, you can attack first. This gives the player who goes first an advantage. In chess, *White always goes first.* For this reason, players choose who will play White. If the players are in a tournament, they will be given the colors they must play by the tournament officials.

Since White moves first, *White has the advantage, so White can take the offense.* This means that White starts as the attacker and Black starts as the defender. White tries to keep this advantage through the whole game.

Since Black moves second, Black's game usually starts as a defensive one. Black must wait to see what White will do. Black tries to take the advantage from White during the course of the game. Black would like to attack while White defends.

REVIEW OF THE CHESSBOARD

Pieces and Pawns

28. What does "light on the right" mean? _____ _____

29. How many squares are on the whole chessboard? _____

30. How do White's pieces line up on the chessboard from left to right at the start of a game? _____ _____

31. What does "Queen on her own color" mean? _____ _____

32. How much is a Bishop worth? _____

33. How much is a Knight worth? _____

34. How much is a Queen worth? _____

35. The Knight moves in the shape of which capital letter? _____

36. How does a Queen move? _____ _____

37. Can Pawns move backward? _____

38. Can Rooks move backward? _____

39. When can a Pawn move ahead two squares? _____

40. Can Kings move to a square two squares away? _____

41. How many Kings are there on a chessboard during a real game? _____

42. Can the Queen jump over other pieces or Pawns? _____

43. Which piece can jump over other pieces or Pawns? _____

44. Are you allowed to let your King be captured? _____

45. If you accidentally move your King to a square where it can be captured, can the enemy take it? _____

46. How many pieces does White have at the start of a chess game? _____ _____

47. How many men does Black have at the start of a chess game? _____ _____

48. Which pieces are minor pieces? _____

49. Which pieces are major pieces? _____

50. What is a rank? _____ _____

51. What is a file? _____ _____

52. What is a diagonal? _____ _____

53. Most of the time, would you rather have a Rook or a Bishop?

_____

54. Most of the time, would you rather have a Queen or a Rook? _____

_____

55. Most of the time, would you rather have a Rook or two Knights?

_____

56. Most of the time, would you rather have a Queen or a Rook and a minor piece? _____

_____

57. Most of the time, would you rather have a Queen or three minor pieces?

_____

58. Most of the time, would you rather have a Queen or two Rooks?

_____

59. Most of the time, would you rather have a Knight or four Pawns?

_____

60. Most of the time, would you rather have a Bishop or two Pawns?

_____

Remember, check your answers with those given in Answers for Chapter 1, pages 179–85.

 CHAPTER 2

Chess Notation

Chess notation is a language invented especially for chess. It helps us to play and learn the game. When we use chess notation, we always know exactly which square we mean, because *every square has its own name*. We have already used these names in Chapter 1. Now we will learn more about them!

Look at Diagram 36. Notice the letters below the squares, going from left to right.

Diagram 36

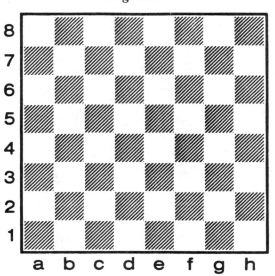

These letters refer to the lines of squares going up the chessboard. These lines are *files*. There are eight files. Their names from left to right are:

the a-file
the b-file
the c-file
the d-file
the e-file
the f-file
the g-file
the h-file

The names of files.

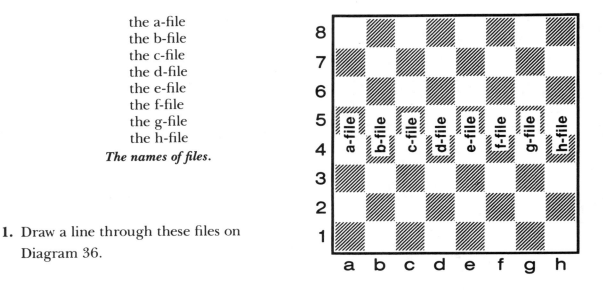

1. Draw a line through these files on Diagram 36.

Look at Diagram 36 again. Notice the numbers written to the left of the squares, going from the bottom to the top.

These numbers refer to the lines of squares going across the chessboard. These lines are *ranks*. There are eight ranks. Going from the top of the diagram to the bottom, the names of the ranks are:

the 8th rank
the 7th rank
the 6th rank
the 5th rank
the 4th rank
the 3rd rank
the 2nd rank
the 1st rank

The names of ranks.

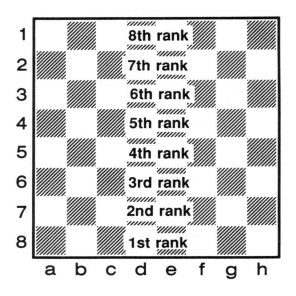

2. Draw a line through these ranks on Diagram 36.

In algebraic chess notation, squares are named by combining the letter of the file with the number of the rank. The file gives the square the first part of its name and the rank gives the square the second part of its name.

Algebraic notation is very easy to learn and is used by today's chess players. There is another, older type of chess notation called descriptive notation. We will talk more about descriptive notation later.

Diagram 37 has some algebraic names already written in.

Diagram 37

3. In Diagram 37, find and circle squares d4; f6; a1; b8; and h5.

4. Where there are blank square boxes in Diagram 37, fill in the name of each square.

5. In Diagram 37, cross off the following blank squares: e4; h7; g2; and a7.

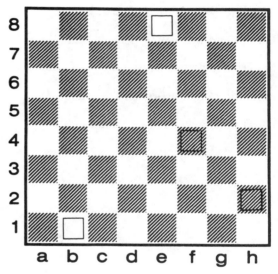

Diagram 38 shows pieces and Pawns on different squares, just as they would be if we were in the middle of a chess game.

In Diagram 38, give the algebraic name for the square where each piece and Pawn sits:

6. The White King _____

7. The Black Queen _____

8. The White Pawn _____

9. The Black Pawn _____

10. The White Bishop _____

11. The Black Knight _____

12. The White Rook _____

13. The Black King _____

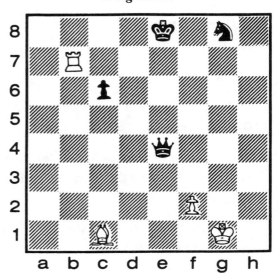

Diagram 38

Diagram 39 shows all the pieces and Pawns sitting on their original squares, as they would at the start of a chess game.

In Diagram 39, give the algebraic names of the squares occupied by:

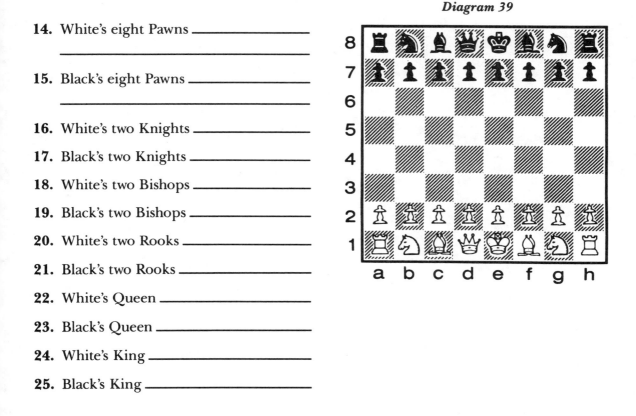

Diagram 39

14. White's eight Pawns _____
_____

15. Black's eight Pawns _____
_____

16. White's two Knights _____

17. Black's two Knights _____

18. White's two Bishops _____

19. Black's two Bishops _____

20. White's two Rooks _____

21. Black's two Rooks _____

22. White's Queen _____

23. Black's Queen _____

24. White's King _____

25. Black's King _____

In chess notation, we use the capital letter K to stand for the word King.

In fact, in chess notation, all the pieces use capital letters to stand for their names. These letters are:

	Chessman	Abbreviation
	King	K
	Queen	Q
	Rook	R
	Bishop	B
	Knight	N
	Pawn	P

A chart of the pieces.

We use the letter N to stand for the Knight so that we do not confuse it with the King.

When we want to show that the Bishop on c1 is moving to e3, we write it this way in algebraic notation: Bc1–e3.

To read Bc1–e3 out loud, we would say, "Bishop on c1 to e3."

There is a shorter form of algebraic notation that leaves out the square on which the chessman starts. Thus Be3 alone, read aloud as "Bishop to e3," means that the Bishop moves to square e3 from whatever square it is on. This shorter form is perfectly clear to experienced chess players, and you will probably go on to use it as you become experienced yourself. However, in this book we will always use the longer form.

Diagram 40

BLACK

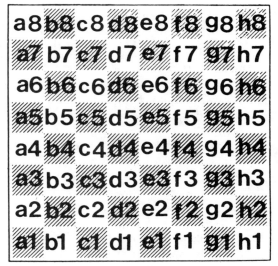

WHITE

26. How would you say Nb1–c3? _____

27. How would you write "Queen on f5 to f8"? _____

28. How would you say Kg8–f8? _____

29. How would you write "Rook on h6 to c6"? _____

30. How would you say Nd6–e4? _____

31. How would you write "Bishop on f8 to g7"? _____

If we wanted to show that the Pawn on e2 is moving to e4, we would write it this way in algebraic notation: e2–e4.

When we want to say this move, we would say: "e2 to e4."

Using a capital letter to stand for a Pawn is not usually necessary, but when it is, we use P. If no letter symbol is given for the chessman that moves, then you know that the moving chessman is a Pawn.

32. How would you say e6–e5? _____

33. How would you write "Pawn on a2 to a4"? _____

34. How would you say h6–h7? _____

35. How would you write "Pawn on d3 to d4"? _____

36. In Diagram 41, set up this position for White, using P for pawn, K for King, and so on:

Pawns on a2, b2, c2, e4, f3, g2, and h2.
Knight on c3.
Bishop on e3.
Rooks on d1 and e1.
Queen on d2.
King on g1.

37. Also in Diagram 41, set up this position for Black:

Pawns on a7, b6, c5, f7, g7, and h7.
Knight on f6.
Bishop on d7.
Rooks on d8 and e6.
Queen on c7.
King on g8.

Diagram 41

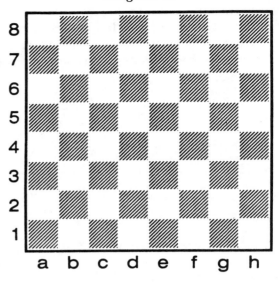

Many times we may want to write down a chess game. We may want to save it to show to our teacher. That way we will find our mistakes and learn not to make them again.

In a tournament, we must write down the moves of our games because the rules require it. When the moves are written down, there is never any doubt about which man is on which square, or whose turn it is. Because the great chess players wrote down their games, we can replay and enjoy those games anytime we want. We can study them and learn from the best.

When we record a game, we write down chess moves. We always write the moves White makes in the left-hand column and the moves Black makes in the right-hand column.

Diagrams 42, 43, 44, and 45 show the opening of a chess game. Here is how these moves are recorded in algebraic notation:

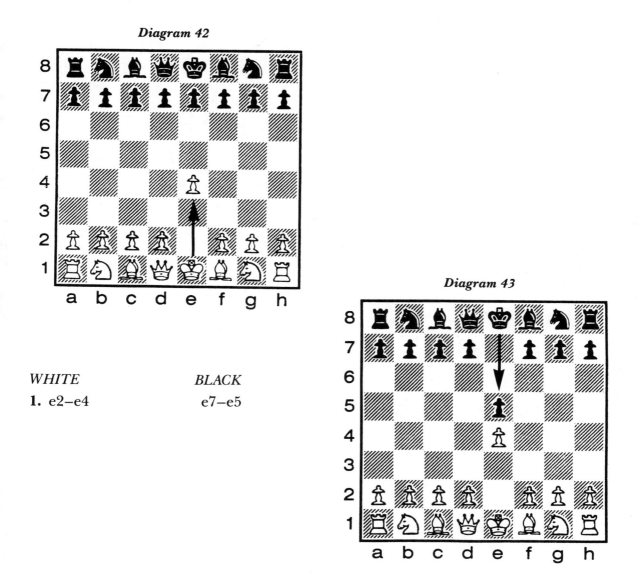

Diagram 42

Diagram 43

WHITE	BLACK
1. e2–e4	e7–e5

This means, on the first move, White moved the Pawn on e2 to e4 and Black moved the pawn on e7 to e5.

The game might go on this way:

Diagram 44

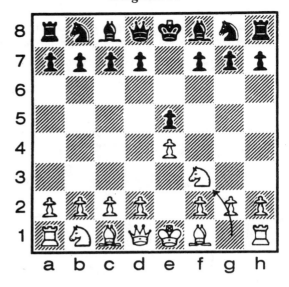

WHITE

2. Ngl–f3

BLACK

Nb8–c6

On the second move, White attacked Black's Pawn on e5, by moving the Knight on g1 to f3. Black answered by defending the Pawn on e5, moving the Knight on b8 to c6.

Diagram 45 gives the position as it now stands.

Diagram 45

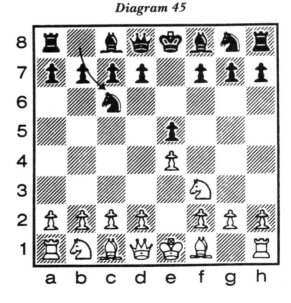

The game might go on this way:

Diagram 46

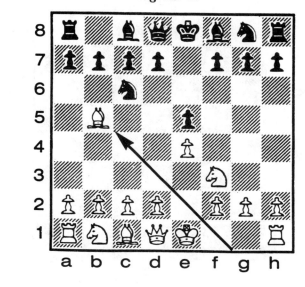

WHITE

3. Bf1–b5

BLACK

d7–d6

On the third move, White moved the Bishop on f1 out to attack Black's Knight at c6. Black moved the Pawn on d7 to d6.

Diagram 47

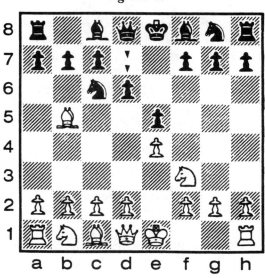

Now we are going to give two new signs. They are × and +.

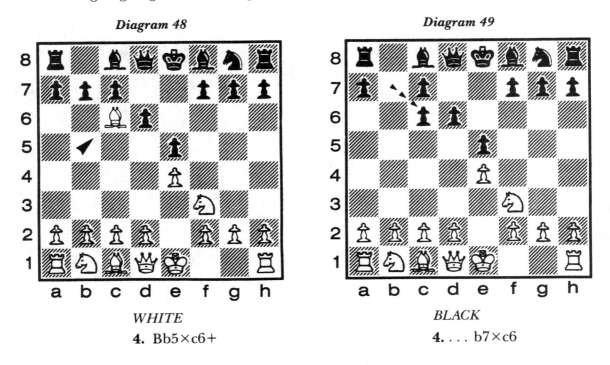

Diagram 48	Diagram 49
WHITE	BLACK
4. Bb5×c6+	4. . . . b7×c6

In chess notation × stands for "takes," or "captures," and + stands for "check," which means "attacks the King." So White's fourth move, 4. Bb5×c6+, means that White's Bishop on b5 took the Black chessman on c6 and checked—that is, attacked—the Black King.

If we read this aloud we would say: "Bishop on b5 takes on c6, check."

Black must then answer the check—that is, protect the King from the White Bishop's attack. So Black takes the Bishop with the Black Pawn on b7, 4. . . . b7×c6. We say: "Pawn on b7 takes on c6."

A Tale of Kings and Queens

The Queen is a very important piece. It stands next to the King on a middle file of the board. It has the most scope and power of all the pieces. One half of the board, the *Queenside*, is named for it.

There is, for example, a Queen-Bishop. It is on the Queenside, right next to the Queen, at the start of the game. White's Queen-Bishop starts on c1 and Black's on c8.

The White Queen-Bishop looks across the board to see the Black

Queen-Bishop looking back. Remember, the Queen starts the game on the square of its color. Since the Bishop sits on the square next to it, then White's Queen-Bishop travels on dark diagonals, and Black's Queen-Bishop travels on light diagonals.

Even though the Queen is very important, when you lose it, you can keep playing. Kings are even more important than Queens. If a King is lost, it is checkmate and the game is over. Since half the board is named for the Queen, the other half is named for the King. This second half is the *Kingside*.

The Pawns on the e-file, f-file, g-file, and h-file are on the Kingside. All the chessmen to the right of the King at the beginning of the game are on the Kingside.

If we can have a Queen-Bishop, we can also have a King-Knight. Look at Diagram 51 and see what you have learned about the Kingside and the Queenside of the chessboard.

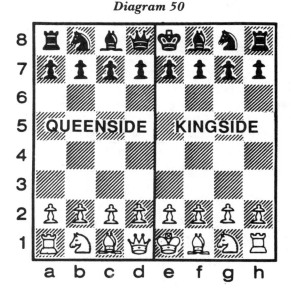

Diagram 50   Diagram 51

38. On which squares do the King-Knights and the King-Rooks start the game? _____

39. On which squares do the Queen-Knights and the Queen-Rooks start the game? _____

40. What is the name of the piece that sits on f1 at the beginning of a game? ____

	Abbreviation	Descriptive Name	Starting Square	Other Names
WHITE'S PIECES	QR	Queen-Rook	a1	
	QN	Queen-Knight	b1	
	QB	Queen-Bishop	c1	dark-square Bishop
	Q	Queen	d1	
	K	King	e1	
	KB	King-Bishop	f1	light-square Bishop
	KN	King-Knight	g1	
	KR	King-Rook	h1	
BLACK'S PIECES	QR	Queen-Rook	a8	
	QN	Queen-Knight	b8	
	QB	Queen-Bishop	c8	light-square Bishop
	Q	Queen	d8	
	K	King	e8	
	KB	King-Bishop	f8	dark-square Bishop
	KN	King-Knight	g8	
	KR	King-Rook	h8	

	Abbreviation	Descriptive Pawn Name	White's Starting Square	Black's Starting Square	Algebraic Pawn Name
WHITE and BLACK	QRP	Queen-Rook Pawn	a2	a7	a-Pawn
	QNP	Queen-Knight Pawn	b2	b7	b-Pawn
	QBP	Queen-Bishop Pawn	c2	c7	c-Pawn
	QP	Queen Pawn	d2	d7	d-Pawn
	KP	King Pawn	e2	e7	e-Pawn
	KBP	King-Bishop Pawn	f2	f7	f-Pawn
	KNP	King-Knight Pawn	g2	g7	g-Pawn
	KRP	King-Rook Pawn	h2	h7	h-Pawn

A chart of names.

More File Names

Every file has two names. We have already learned the algebraic names of the files. Starting on White's left-hand side, they are the a-file, the b-file, the c-file, the d-file, the e-file, the f-file, the g-file, and the h-file.

The other names for files come from the pieces sitting on them at the start of a game. Because both White and Black have their Queen-Rooks on the a-file at the start of the game, the a-file is also called the Queen-Rook file.

The a-file keeps this descriptive name, the Queen-Rook file, even if the Queen-Rooks are later moved to the Kingside. All the file names stay the same no matter where the pieces for which the files are named go.

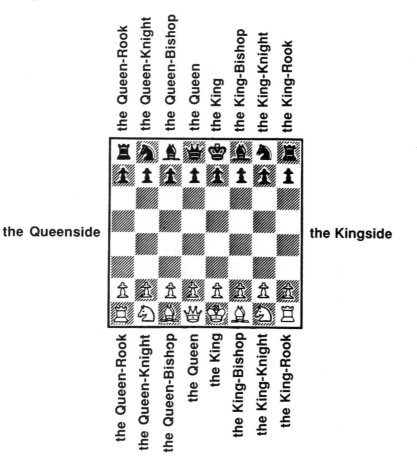

Descriptive names of files.

The b-file is also called the Queen-Knight file, because the Queen-Knights for both sides start the game on the b-file.

The table shows the two names for each file.

Remember: *File names using numbers and small letters are algebraic names. File names using the names of chess pieces are descriptive names.*

Fill in the blanks:

Algebraic Name		Descriptive Name
41. _____	is also	the Queen-Rook file.
42. The b-file	is also	_____.
43. _____	is also	the Queen-Bishop file.
44. The d-file	is also	_____.
45. _____	is also	the King-file.
46. The f-file	is also	_____.
47. _____	is also	the King-Knight file.
48. The h-file	is also	_____.

The Names of Pawns

Pawns have names, too. If a Pawn's starting square is on the a-file, we call it an a-Pawn. If it starts on a2, it is White's a-Pawn. If it starts on a7, it is Black's a-Pawn. The names of the Pawns are the same for White and Black. They are:

PAWN NAMES	STARTING SQUARES	
	White	Black
a-Pawn	a2	a7
b-Pawn	b2	b7
c-Pawn	c2	c7
d-Pawn	d2	d7
e-Pawn	e2	e7
f-Pawn	f2	f7
g-Pawn	g2	g7
h-Pawn	h2	h7

The Pawns are also given descriptive names. They are named by which side of the board they start on and by the piece that sits behind them.

Diagram 52

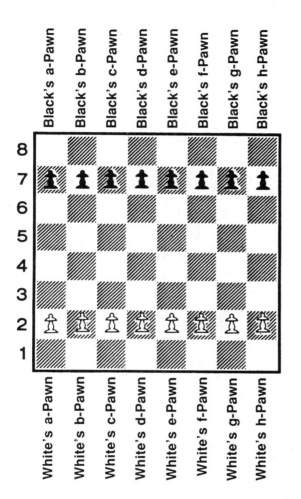

Diagram 53 shows the names of the Pawns written in. The b-Pawn on b2 is White's Queen-Knight Pawn, because it starts on the Queen-side, in front of the Queen-Knight.

Diagram 53

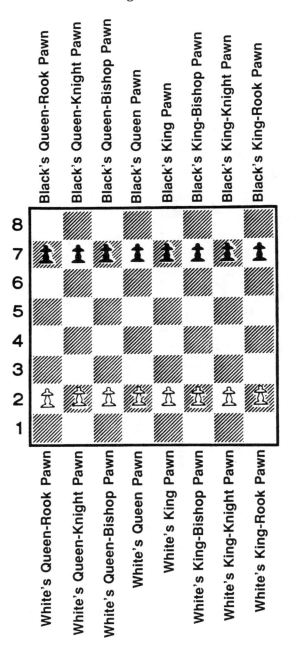

The g-Pawn on g7 is Black's King-Knight Pawn, because it starts on Black's Kingside, in front of the King-Knight.

The h-Pawn on h2 is White's King-Rook Pawn, because it starts the game on the Kingside, in front of the King-Rook.

Give both names for the other Pawns:

49. The Pawn on a2:

        algebraic name:_____

        descriptive name:_____

50. The Pawn on c2:

        algebraic name:_____

        descriptive name:_____

51. The Pawn on d2:

        algebraic name:_____

        descriptive name:_____

52. The Pawn on e2:

        algebraic name:_____

        descriptive name:_____

53. The Pawn on f2:

        algebraic name:_____

        descriptive name:_____

54. The Pawn on g2:

        algebraic name:_____

        descriptive name:_____

55. The Pawn on a7:

        algebraic name:_____

        descriptive name:_____

56. The Pawn on b7:

        algebraic name:_____

        descriptive name:_____

57. The Pawn on c7:

        algebraic name:_____

        descriptive name:_____

58. The Pawn on d7:

     algebraic name:_____

     descriptive name:_____

59. The Pawn on e7:

     algebraic name:_____

     descriptive name:_____

60. The Pawn on f7:

     algebraic name:_____

     descriptive name:_____

61. The Pawn on h7:

     algebraic name:_____

     descriptive name:_____

No matter what happens in the game, the Bishop starting on b8 will always be Black's Queen-Bishop. Even if it moves to h3, which is on the Kingside, it will still be the Queen-Bishop. It is easy to identify, because it is always on a light square, whereas Black's King-Bishop is always on a dark square.

We don't use descriptive names that much for Rooks and Knights once they've moved, because it might be hard to remember on which side of the board the piece started the game.

The names of the Pawns change if they move to another file by a capture. If a Pawn never captures a piece or another Pawn, it stays on the same file for the whole game and keeps the same name. But if the a-Pawn takes a man on the b-file, it moves to the b-file and becomes a b-pawn. The descriptive name changes, too. If White's King-Rook Pawn takes something on the g-file, it becomes a King-Knight Pawn.

So, in Diagram 54, if the King-Rook Pawn takes the Black Knight,
White will have two King-Knight Pawns and no King-Rook Pawn.

Diagram 54

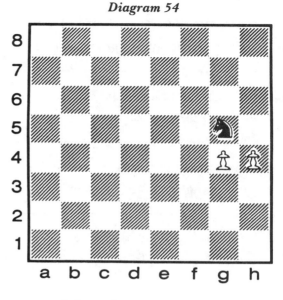

See what you have learned about Pawns' names and how they
capture. Diagram 55 shows doubled g-Pawns. White got the extra
g-pawn when the h-pawn captured a Black piece on g5.

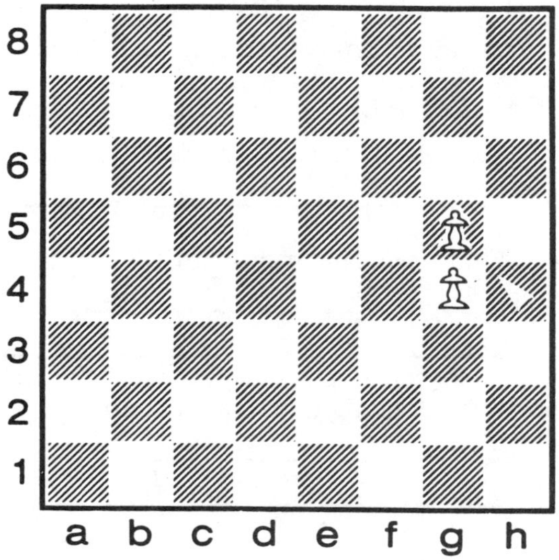

62. Circle the algebraic name of the file in Diagram 55 with the doubled Pawns made by pawn capture:

f-file   a-file   d-file   h-file   g-file

63. Circle the descriptive name for this file:

King-Bishop   Queen-Rook   Queen
     King-Rook   King-Knight

64. What is the algebraic name for the file that used to have the g5-Pawn on it in Diagram 55? _____

_____

65. What is the descriptive name for this file? _____

Diagram 55

REVIEW OF CHESS NOTATION

66. Does every square have a name?
_____

67. How does the square get its name?
_____

68. What is the name of the square the White Queen sits on at the start of a chess game? _____

69. What is the name of the square the Black King sits on at the start of a chess game? _____

70. What are the rows of squares going across the board from left to right called? _____

71. Name the ranks. _____
_____

72. What are the rows of squares going up and down the chessboard from bottom to top called? _____

73. Name the files. _____
_____
_____

74. What does N stand for in chess notation? _____
_____

75. What does B stand for in chess notation? _____
_____

76. What does Q stand for in chess notation? _____
_____

77. What do you write to indicate a Rook in chess notation? _____

78. What do you write to indicate a King in chess notation? _____

79. Is it always necessary to use a P to stand for Pawn in chess notation? _____

80. What does × stand for in chess notation? _____
_____

81. What does + stand for in chess notation? _____
_____

82. Are White's moves written in the right-hand or left-hand column in chess notation? _____

83. Where are Black's moves written in chess notation? _____
_____

84. How would you write "Knight on b1 to c3" in chess notation? _____

85. How would you say c5×Rd4?
_____

86. Mark an X through the Kingside of Diagram 56.

87. Circle White's Queen-Rook in Diagram 56.

88. Give the algebraic name for the square on which it sits. _____

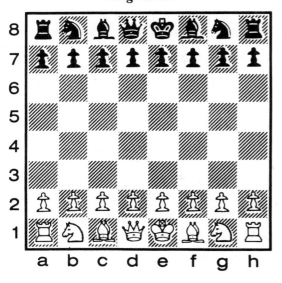

Diagram 56

89. On which square is Black's Queen-Bishop in Diagram 56?

90. Give the algebraic name for the square on which it sits. _____

91. Circle White's Queen-Knight Pawn in Diagram 56.

92. Give the algebraic name for the square on which it sits. _____

93. What is the algebraic name for this Pawn? _____

94. Circle Black's Queen-Rook Pawn in Diagram 56. _____

95. Give the algebraic name for the square on which it sits. _____

96. What is the algebraic name for this Pawn? _____

Check your answers with those given in Answers for Chapter 2, pages 186–89.

CHAPTER 3

Attacks

The words "attack" and "threaten" have chess meanings that are different from their usual meanings. A piece or pawn is *attacked* when it can be captured next move, whether the capture is good or bad. A piece or pawn is *threatened* when it can be captured next move with advantage. Not all captures are good. All threats are attacks, but not all attacks are threats. In chess, we want to capture enemy men without losing any of our own men. We like to capture more valuable men with less valuable men. We also want to save our own men from capture.

In each of the following ten diagrams (Diagrams 57 to 66) there is a Black piece or Pawn that can be attacked if you make the right move. See if you can find it.

Diagram 57

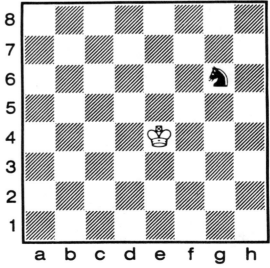

1. In Diagram 57, find White's King and name its square. _____

2. Find Black's Knight and name its square. _____

3. Does White's King threaten Black's Knight? _____

4. Where must the King go to threaten the Knight? _____

5. In Diagram 58, where is White's Bishop? _____

6. Where is Black's Rook? _____

7. Does White's Bishop threaten Black's Rook? _____

8. Where must the Bishop go to threaten the Rook? _____

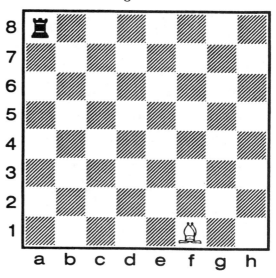

Diagram 58

9. In Diagram 59, find White's Rook and name its square. _____

10. Find Black's Pawn and name its square. _____

11. Does White's Rook threaten Black's Pawn? _____

12. Where must the Rook go to threaten the Pawn? _____

Diagram 59

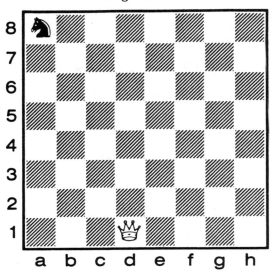

Diagram 60

13. In Diagram 60, find White's Queen and name its square. _____

14. Find Black's Knight and name its square. _____

15. Does White's Queen threaten Black's Knight? _____

16. Where does the Queen go to threaten and *trap* the Knight? _____

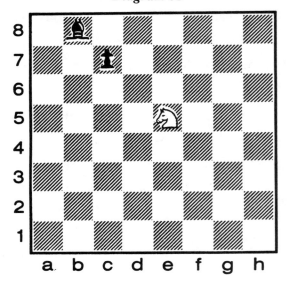

Diagram 61

17. In Diagram 61, find White's Knight and name its square. _____

18. Find Black's Bishop and name its square. _____

19. Does White's Knight threaten Black's Bishop? _____

20. Where must the Knight go to threaten and *trap* the Bishop? _____

21. In Diagram 62, find White's Pawn and name its square. _____

22. Find Black's Rook and name its square. _____

23. Does White's Pawn threaten Black's Rook? _____

24. Where must the Pawn go to attack the Rook? _____

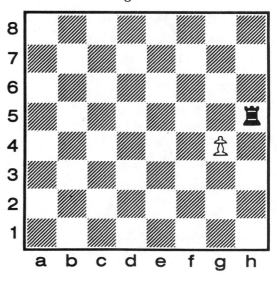

Diagram 62

25. In Diagram 63, White's Bishop can threaten Black's Rook from two squares. What are these squares?

_____

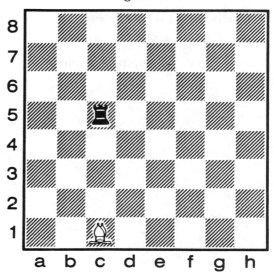

Diagram 63

26. In Diagram 64, White's Rook can threaten Black's Pawn from two squares. What are these squares?

_____

Diagram 64

27. In Diagram 65, White's Knight can threaten Black's Queen from two squares. What are these squares?

_____

Diagram 65

28. In Diagram 66, White's Queen can threaten Black's Knight from five squares. What are these squares?

_____

Diagram 66

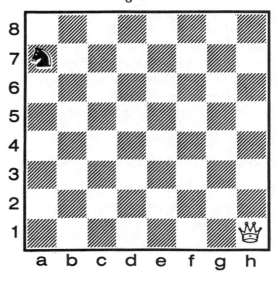

Your Bishop is attacked! Your opponent's Rook is right next to it. Unless you act quickly, your Bishop will be captured on the next move. What should you do?

Diagram 67 shows a Rook threat to your Bishop. Remember: A piece or pawn is threatened when it can be captured with advantage next move. You must save your Bishop.

There may be as many as three ways to save an attacked man. Depending on the situation, you might do any of these:

1. *Move the attacked piece or Pawn* to a safe square.
2. *Block the attack* by moving another man between the attacker and the attacked man.
3. *Capture the attacker.*

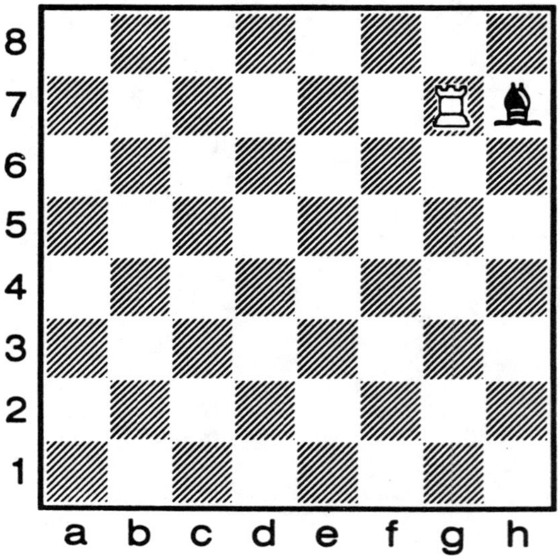

29. In Diagram 67, which of these three methods lets Black save the attacked Bishop?

Diagram 67

If a chessman is attacked by an enemy man of the same value, a trade is possible. When chessmen of equal value are traded, no material is lost and no material is won. When you lose a chessman, try to get back at least as much as you give up.

Remember:

Pawn	=	P	=	1
Knight	=	K	=	3
Bishop	=	B	=	3
Rook	=	R	=	5
Queen	=	Q	=	9

30. In Diagram 68, a chessman is being threatened. Is the threatened chessman Black or White?

_____

31. What is the name of the square where the threatened man sits?

_____

32. What is the value of the threatened man? _____

33. Which piece or Pawn is the attacker?

_____

34. What is the name of the square where the attacker sits? _____

35. What is the value of the attacker?

_____

36. Can the threatened man be saved?

_____

37. How can the threatened piece or Pawn be saved? _____

38. Should the threatened piece or Pawn be saved? _____

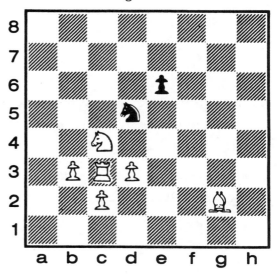

Diagram 68

In chess, *we must think ahead* to future moves. This way we can plan to attack the enemy or avoid the enemy's attack on us.

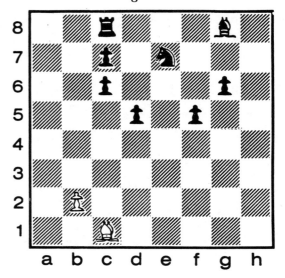

Diagram 69

39. In Diagram 69, can the White Bishop be moved into position to threaten the Black Knight? _____

40. Where must the Bishop go to threaten the Knight? _____

41. Can the Black Knight be protected? _____

42. How much is the Bishop worth? _____

43. How much is the Knight worth? _____

44. Does either side come out behind in a trade of the Bishop for the Knight? _____

45. Look at Diagram 70 very carefully. How can the White Bishop on d3 be moved to threaten the Black Pawn on d6? _____

_____

46. How can the same White Bishop be moved to threaten the Rook on a8? _____

47. Which is worth more, the Rook or the Bishop? _____

48. Can the Rook be saved? _____

Diagram 70

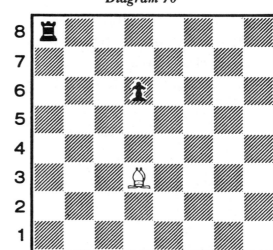

49. In Diagram 71, it is Black's move. Is a Black Pawn under attack? _____

50. Which piece or Pawn is threatening it? _____

51. Can the Pawn be protected? _____

52. How can the Pawn be protected? _____

Diagram 71

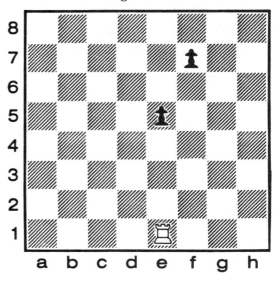

53. In Diagram 72, it is Black's move. What man is the attacker and how can the attacked man be saved? _____

_____

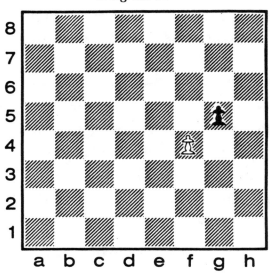

Diagram 72

54. In Diagram 73, it is Black's move. What man is the attacker and how can the attacked man be saved? _____

_____

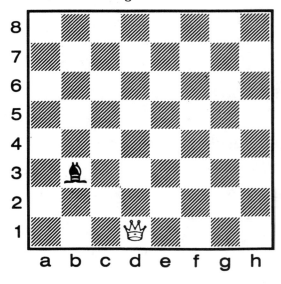

Diagram 73

Diagram 74

55. In Diagram 74, it is Black's move. What man is the attacker and how can the attacked man be saved? _____

_____

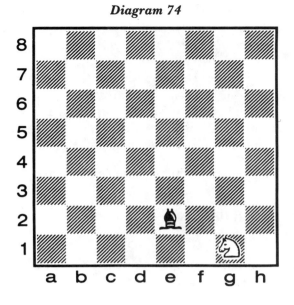

56. In Diagram 75, it is Black's move. What man is the attacker and how can the attacked man be saved? _____

_____

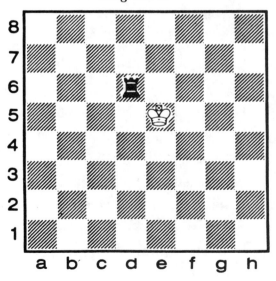

Diagram 75

In Diagram 76, your Black Queen is being threatened by the White Bishop. Unless you act quickly, you will lose your Queen on the next move. The Bishop will simply capture it. The Queen is your most valuable piece and you want to save it. You cannot just move the Queen out of the way, because that would leave the Black King under attack—it is actually against the rules to allow your King to be captured. You could take the Bishop with your Queen, but then the White Knight on c3 could take your Queen—a very poor bargain. So what can you do?

57. Is there another piece or Pawn you can move between your Black Queen and the attacking Bishop?

_____

58. What is the name of the square on which this man sits? _____

59. What is the value of this soldier.

_____

60. What is the name of the square where this chessman could be moved to defend the Queen? _____

61. Can the blocking chessman be captured by the Bishop? _____

62. Which chessman is worth more, the blocking defender of the Queen or the attacking Bishop? _____

63. Is the chessman that blocks the attack to the Queen protected on its new square? _____

64. Can White afford to capture the blocker? _____

65. Why? _____

66. Could the Queen safely recapture on c6 after the Bishop took there?

_____

Diagram 76

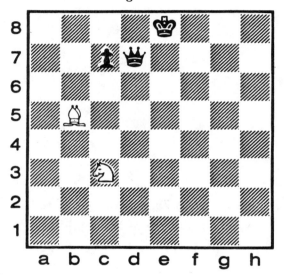

In Diagrams 77 to 82, one piece or Pawn is attacking another. You are to:

- find which chessman is attacked and name its square,
- find which chessman is the attacker and name its square,
- find which chessman can block the attack, and
- name the square to which the blocker must move to defend the attacked chessman.

67. Attacked man and its square in Diagram 77: _____

_____

68. Attacker and its square: _____

_____

69. Chessman that can block the attack:

_____

70. Square where the defender must move: _____

_____

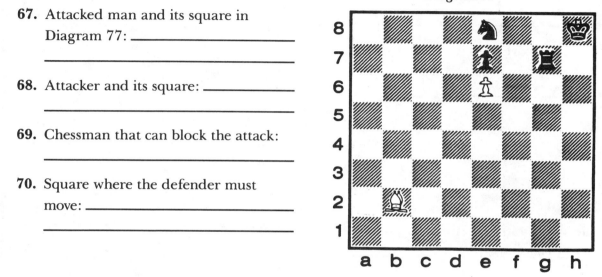

Diagram 77

71. Attacked man and its square in Diagram 78: _____

_____

72. Attacker and its square: _____

_____

73. Chessman that can block the attack:

_____

74. Square where the defender must move: _____

_____

Diagram 78

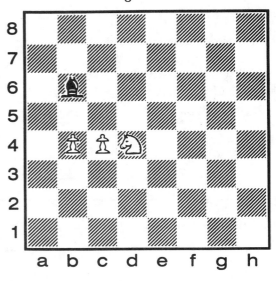

Diagram 79

75. Attacked man and its square in Diagram 79: _____

_____

76. Attacker and its square: _____

_____

77. Chessman that can block the attack:

_____

78. Square where the defender must move: _____

_____

Diagram 80

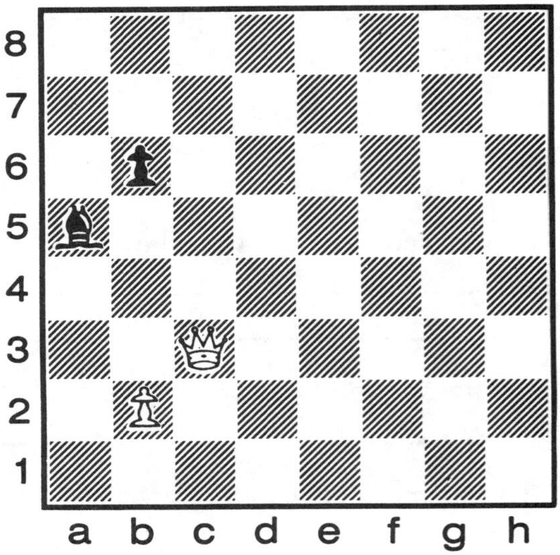

79. White's attacked man and its square in Diagram 80: _____

_____

80. Attacker and its square: _____

_____

81. Chessman that can block the attack:

_____

82. Square where the defender must move: _____

_____

83. Attacked man and its square in Diagram 81: _____

_____

84. Attacker and its square: _____

_____

85. Chessman that can block the attack:

_____

86. Square where the defender must move: _____

_____

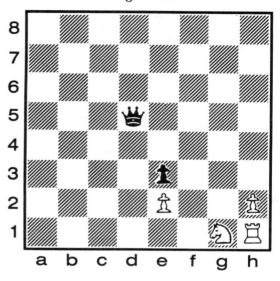

Diagram 81

87. Attacked man and its square in Diagram 82: _____

_____

88. Attacker and its square: _____

_____

89. Chessman that can block the attack:

_____

90. Square where the defender must move: _____

_____

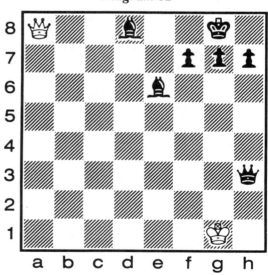

Diagram 82

In Diagram 83, your Black Rook is being attacked by an enemy man. Unless you act quickly, you will lose your Rook on the next move. The Rook is a valuable piece and you want to save it. What can you do?

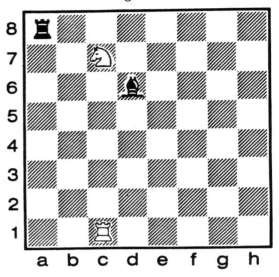

Diagram 83

91. Which piece or Pawn is attacking your Rook? _____

92. On which square does the attacker sit? _____

93. Is there a piece or Pawn protecting the attacker? _____

94. Can you capture the attacking piece or Pawn? _____

95. What is the value of the attacking piece or Pawn? _____

96. Will you win any material—that is, gain any points—by capturing the attacker? _____

97. Why? _____
   _____

98. If you capture the attacker, will your Rook be safe? _____

In Diagrams 84 to 89, one piece or Pawn is attacking another. You are to:

- find which piece or Pawn is attacked and name its square,
- find which piece or Pawn is the attacker and name its square,
- see if you can capture the attacker safely (that is, come out ahead),
- see if you will gain points by capturing the attacker.

99. White's threatened man and its square in Diagram 84: _____

_____

100. Attacker and its square: _____

_____

101. Can you capture the attacker and come out ahead? _____

_____

102. Will you win material? _____

_____

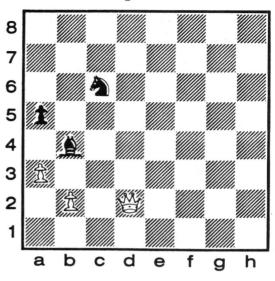

Diagram 84

103. Black's threatened man and its square in Diagram 85: _____

_____

104. Attacker and its square: _____

_____

105. Can you capture the attacker and come out ahead? _____

_____

106. Will you win material? _____

_____

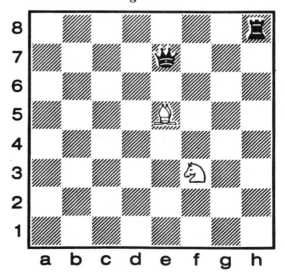

Diagram 85

107. White's threatened man and its square in Diagram 86: _____

_____

108. Attacker and its square: _____

_____

109. Can you capture the attacker and come out ahead? _____

_____

110. Will you win material? _____

_____

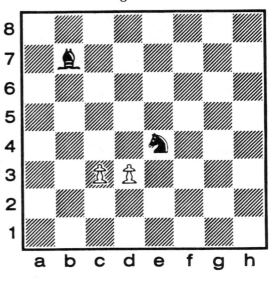

Diagram 86

111. Black's threatened man and its square in Diagram 87: _____

_____

112. Attacker and square: _____

_____

113. Can you capture the attacker and come out ahead? _____

_____

114. Will you win material? _____

_____

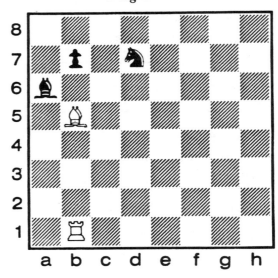

Diagram 87

115. Black's threatened man and its square in Diagram 88: _____

_____

116. Attacker and its square: _____

_____

117. Can you capture the attacker and come out ahead? _____

_____

118. Will you win material? _____

_____

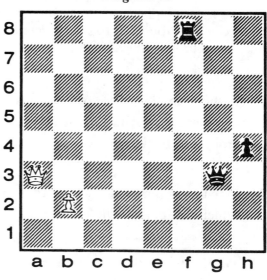

Diagram 88

119. White's threatened man and its square in Diagram 89: _____

_____

120. Attacker and its square: _____

_____

121. Can you capture the attacker and come out ahead? _____

_____

122. Will you win material? _____

_____

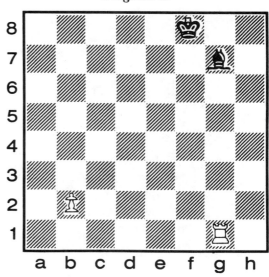

Diagram 89

In Diagram 90, your Black Knight is being threatened by an enemy Queen. Unless you act quickly, you will lose your Knight on the next move. You want to save it. Besides just moving it away, what can you do to save the Knight?

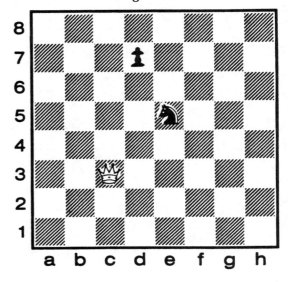

Diagram 90

123. Is there another piece or Pawn you can move to defend your Knight from the attacking Queen?

_____

124. What is the name of the square on which this possible defender now sits? _____

125. Where should this chessman go to defend the Knight? _____

In Diagrams 91 to 96 one piece or Pawn is attacking another. You are to:

- find which piece or Pawn is attacked and name its square,
- find which piece or Pawn is the attacker and name its square,
- find which piece or Pawn can defend the attacked chessman, and
- name the square to which the defender must move to protect the attacked chessman.

126. Black's threatened man and its square in Diagram 91: _____

_____

127. Attacker and its square: _____

_____

128. Man that can defend the threatened chessman: _____

_____

129. Square to which the defender must move: _____

_____

Diagram 91

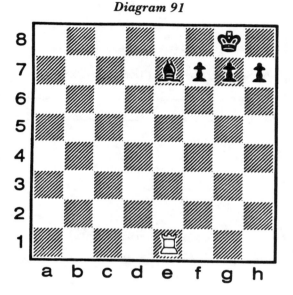

130. Black's threatened man and its square in Diagram 92: _____

_____

131. Attacker and its square: _____

_____

132. Man that can defend the threatened chessman: _____

_____

133. Square to which the defender must move: _____

_____

Diagram 92

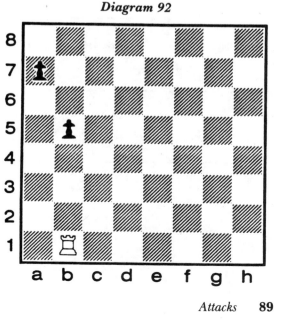

134. Black's threatened man and its square in Diagram 93: _____

_____

135. Attacker and its square: _____

_____

136. Man that can defend the threatened chessman: _____

_____

137. Square to which the defender must move: _____

_____

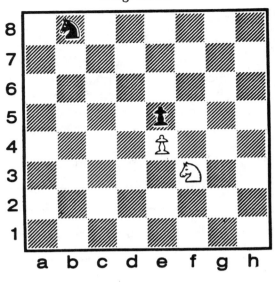

Diagram 93

138. White's threatened man and its square in Diagram 94: _____

_____

139. Attacker and its square: _____

_____

140. Man that can defend the threatened chessman: _____

_____

141. Square to which the attacked man must move to be safe: _____

_____

Diagram 94

142. White's threatened man and its square in Diagram 95: _____

_____

143. Attacker and its square: _____

_____

144. Man that can defend the threatened chessman: _____

_____

145. Square to which the defender must move: _____

_____

Diagram 95

146. White's threatened man and its square in Diagram 96: _____

_____

147. Attacker and its square: _____

_____

148. Man that can defend the threatened chessman: _____

_____

149. Square to which the defender must move: _____

_____

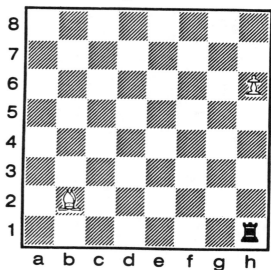

Diagram 96

REVIEW OF ATTACKS

150. What is an attack? _____
_____

151. What is a trade? _____
_____

152. Can you save an attacked man by moving it? _____

153. Can you save an attacked man by blocking the attack? _____

154. Can you save an attacked man by capturing the attacker? _____
_____

155. Can you save an attacked man by defending it? _____

156. Do you lose material in a trade? _____

157. Can you win material by capturing an attacker? _____

Check your answers with those given in Answers for Chapter 3, pages 190–206.

CHAPTER 4

Check

Black is attacking one of White's pieces in Diagram 97. But there is something special about this attack. Can you see how this attack is different from those of Chapter 3?

Diagram 97

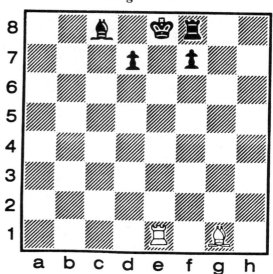

1. Which one of White's pieces in Diagram 97 is the attacker, and what is the name of the square where the attacker sits? _____

2. Which Black piece is under attack? _____

3. How can the Black piece escape the attack? _____

This kind of attack has a very special name. It is *check*. When the King is under attack and might be captured on the next move, we say *the King is in check.*

When the King is in check, it must be saved. The King can *never* be captured or traded. *If the King cannot be saved, the game is over.* If your King is in check, you cannot make any other move before you save it. If the enemy King is in check, it, too, must be saved before any other move is made.

When the King is in check, it can be saved (gotten out of check) in the same ways as any attacked piece or Pawn could be saved: (1) by moving it to a safe square, (2) by moving another man in the way, or (3) by capturing the attacker.

In Diagrams 98 to 103, the White King may be in check. You are to find out if the King is in check, name the piece that is giving check to the White King and name its square, and see if the King can escape the check.

4. In Diagram 98, is the White King in check? _____

5. Which Black piece or Pawn is giving check, and what is its square?

_____

6. How can White escape the check?

_____

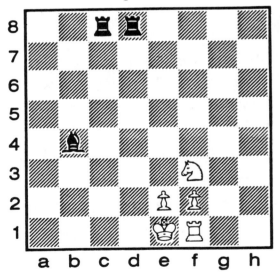

Diagram 98

7. In Diagram 99, is the White King in check? _____

8. Which Black piece or Pawn is giving check, and what is its square? _____

9. How can White escape the check? _____

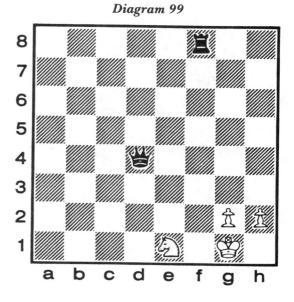

Diagram 99

10. In Diagram 100, is the White King in check? _____

11. Which Black piece or Pawn is giving check, and what is its square? _____

12. How can White escape the check? _____

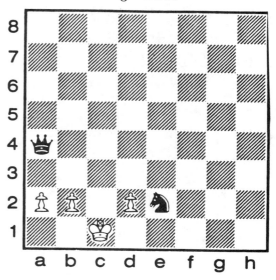

Diagram 100

13. In Diagram 101, is the White King in check? _____

14. Which Black piece or Pawn is giving check, and what is its square? _____

15. How can White escape the check? Or, if White is not in check, what move should White make? _____

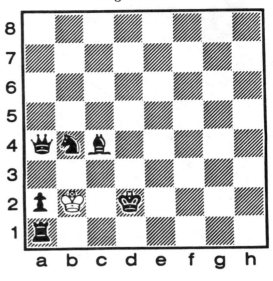

Diagram 101

16. In Diagram 102, is the White King in check? _____

17. Which Black piece or Pawn is giving check, and what is its square? _____

18. How can White escape the check? _____

Diagram 102

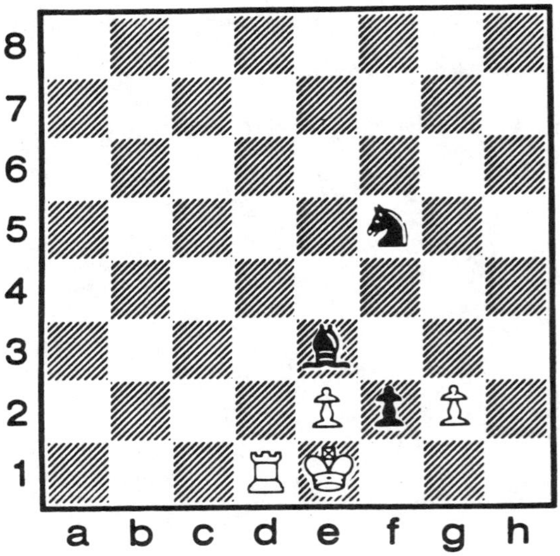

19. In Diagram 103, is the White King in check? _____

20. Which Black piece or Pawn is giving check, and what is its square?

_____

21. How can White escape the check?

_____

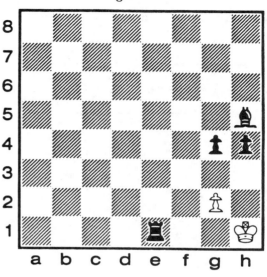

Diagram 103

Diagrams 104 to 107 show some similar problems for Black. See if you can find a safe square for the Black King.

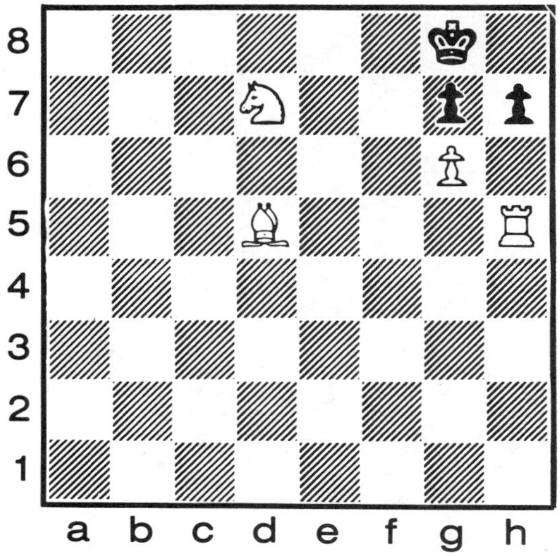

22. White attacker and its square in Diagram 104: _____

_____

23. Black King's safe square: _____

_____

Diagram 104

24. White attacker and its square in Diagram 105: _____

_____

25. Black King's safe square: _____

_____

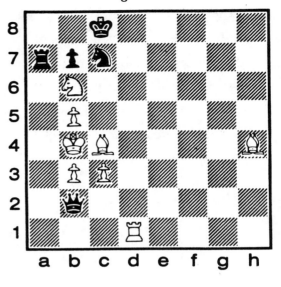

Diagram 105

26. White attacker and its square in Diagram 106: _____

_____

27. Black King's safe square: _____

_____

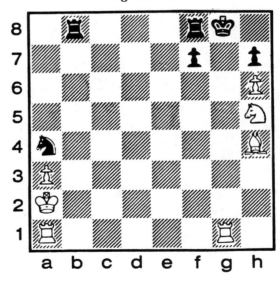

Diagram 106

Diagram 107

28. White attacker and its square in
Diagram 107: _____

_____

29. Black King's safe square: _____

_____

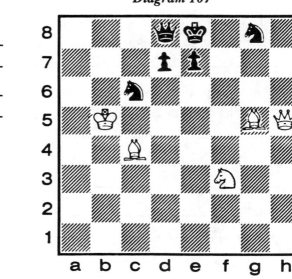

Sometimes there is no safe square where the King can move. But it may still be possible to block the attack by putting another piece or Pawn between the attacker and the King.

In Diagrams 108 to 113, one of the Kings may be in check. You are to:

- find out if either White's King or Black's King is in check and name its square,
- find out which piece or Pawn is giving check to the King and name its square,
- see if the check to the King can be blocked, and tell which piece or Pawn can do the blocking.

Diagram 108

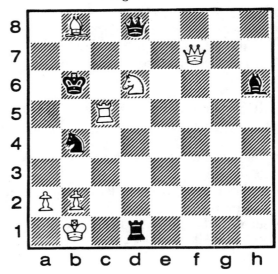

30. In Diagram 108, which King is in check and what is its square? ———

———

31. What chessman is giving check and what is its square? ———

———

32. Can the attack be blocked? ———

———

33. How? ———

———

Diagram 109

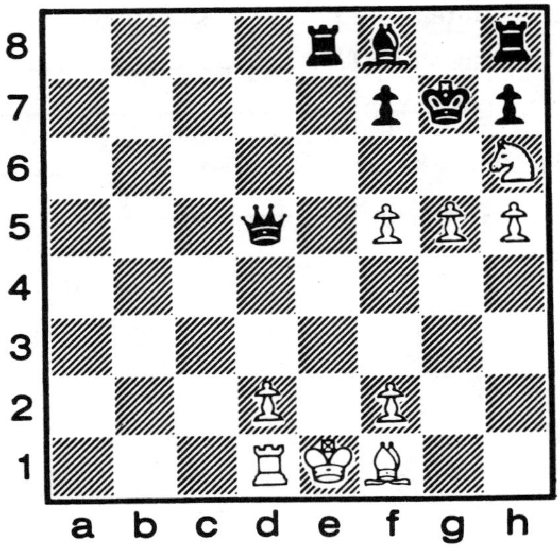

34. In Diagram 109, which King in check and what is its square? ———

———

35. What chessman is giving check and what is its square? ———

———

36. Can the attack be blocked? ———

———

37. How? ———

———

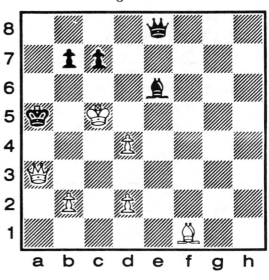

Diagram 110

38. In Diagram 110, which King is in check and what is its square? _____

_____

39. What chessman is giving check and what is its square? _____

_____

40. Can the attack be blocked? _____

_____

41. How? _____

_____

Diagram 111

42. In Diagram 111, which King is in check and what is its square? _____

_____

43. What chessman is giving check and what is its square? _____

_____

44. Can the attack be blocked? _____

_____

45. How? _____

_____

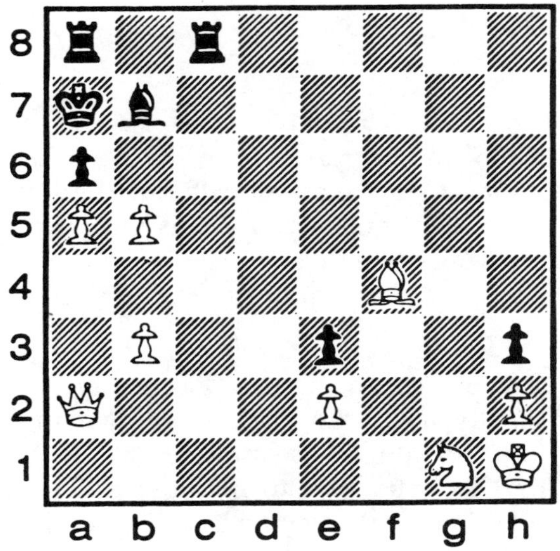

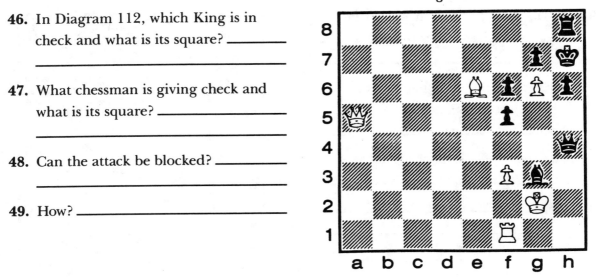

Diagram 112

46. In Diagram 112, which King is in check and what is its square? _____

_____

47. What chessman is giving check and what is its square? _____

_____

48. Can the attack be blocked? _____

_____

49. How? _____

Help! In Diagrams 113 to 117, your White King is in check. If you do not act right now, you will lose the game. Maybe you can take the enemy piece or Pawn that has put your King in check. Then your King would be safe again.

Here you have a lot of things to do. You must

- find out which piece or Pawn is giving check to the White King,
- see if you can capture the enemy man,
- find the value of the attacker,
- find the value of your man that will capture it,
- see whether the enemy can take you back, and,
- if the enemy can take you back, figure out if you will gain material.

50. In Diagram 113, which man of Black's is giving check and what is its square? _____

_____

51. Which man of White's can capture the enemy? _____

_____

52. What are the values of the enemy and the defender? _____

_____

53. Can the enemy take back? _____

_____

54. Will you gain or lose material? _____

_____

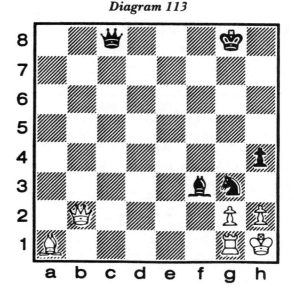

Diagram 113

55. In Diagram 114, which man of Black's is giving check and what is its square? _____

_____

56. Which of White's men can capture the enemy? _____

_____

57. What are the values of the enemy and the defender? _____

_____

58. Can the enemy take back? _____

_____

59. Will you gain or lose material? _____

_____

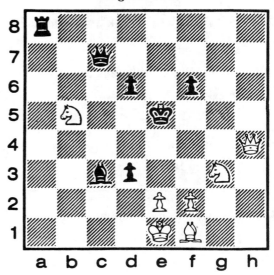

Diagram 114

60. In Diagram 115, which man of Black's is giving check and what is its square? _____

_____

61. Which man of White's can capture the enemy? _____

62. What are the values of the enemy and the defender? _____

_____

63. Can the enemy take back? _____

_____

64. Will you gain or lose material?

_____

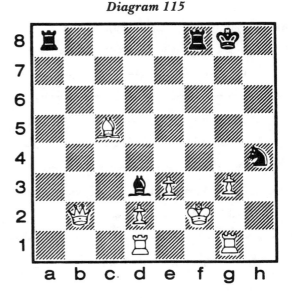

Diagram 115

65. In Diagram 116, which man of Black's is giving check and what is its square? _____

66. Which man of White's can capture the enemy? _____

_____

67. What are the values of the enemy and the defender? _____

_____

68. Can the enemy take back? _____

_____

69. Will you gain or lose material? _____

_____

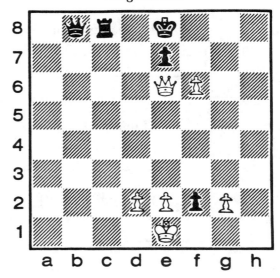

Diagram 116

70. In Diagram 117, which man of Black's is giving check and what is its square? _____

_____

71. Which man of White's can capture the enemy? _____

_____

72. What are the values of the enemy and the defender? _____

_____

73. Can the enemy take back? _____

_____

74. Will you gain or lose material? _____

_____

Diagram 117

75. In Diagram 118, which man of Black's is giving check and what is its square? _____

_____

76. Which man of White's can capture the enemy? _____

_____

77. What are the values of the enemy and the defender? _____

_____

78. Can the enemy take back? _____

_____

79. Will you gain or lose material? _____

_____

Diagram 118

In Diagrams 119 to 123, you are White and you think you see your big chance. If you make the right move, maybe you can put the Black King in check.

Diagram 119

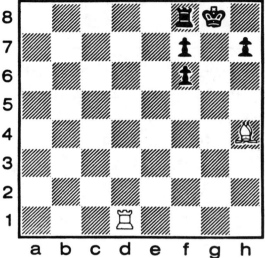

80. In Diagram 119, can you check the Black King? _____

_____

81. With what man? _____

_____

82. How? _____

_____

Diagram 120

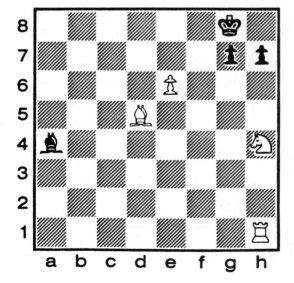

83. In Diagram 120, can you check the Black King? _____

_____

84. With what man? _____

_____

85. How? _____

_____

86. In Diagram 121, can you check the Black King? _____

_____

87. With what man? _____

_____

88. How? _____

_____

Diagram 121

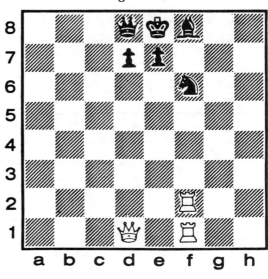

89. In Diagram 122, can you check the Black King? _____

_____

90. With what man? _____

_____

91. How? _____

_____

Diagram 122

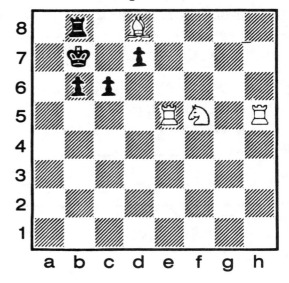

Diagram 123

92. In Diagram 123, can you check the Black King? _____

_____

93. With what man? _____

_____

94. How? _____

_____

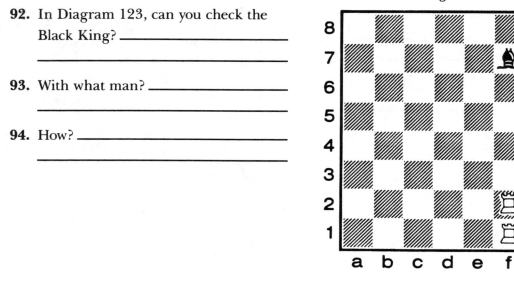

Holy Moley! in Diagrams 124 to 128, you are White and you think you see your big chance. If you make the right move, maybe you can put the Black King in check. But you must use the piece or Pawn named in the diagram.

Diagram 124

95. In Diagram 124, using the White Pawn on g6, can you give check on the next move? _____

96. How? _____

_____

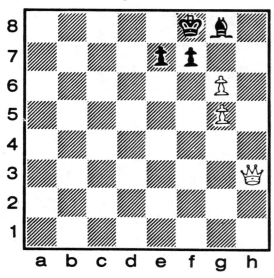

97. In Diagram 125, using the White Rook on f1, can you give check on the next move? _____

_____

98. How? _____

_____

Diagram 125

99. In Diagram 126, using the White Knight on e5, can you give check on the next move? _____

_____

100. How? _____

_____

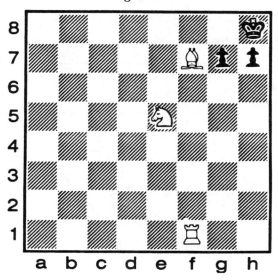

Diagram 126

Diagram 127

101. In Diagram 127, using the White Bishop on c1, can you give check on the next move? _____

_____

102. How? _____

_____

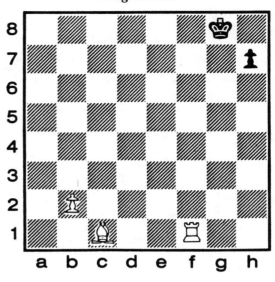

Diagram 128

103. In Diagram 128, using the Queen on e2, can you give check on the next move? _____

_____

104. How? _____

_____

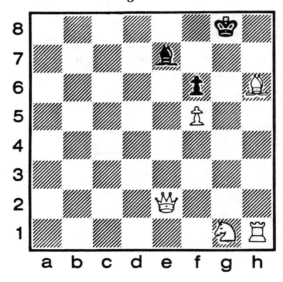

Oh, no! In Diagrams 129 to 133, your Black King is in check. You must see how you can save it, or you will lose the game on the next move. You are to find out which White piece or Pawn is giving check and then decide whether the way to get out of check is to block the check, move your King, or capture the attacker.

105. In Diagram 129, which man of White's on what square is giving check? _____

106. Can Black block the check, move the King, or capture the attacker?

_____

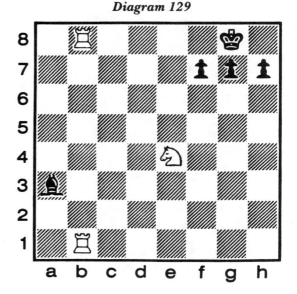

Diagram 129

107. In Diagram 130, which man of White's on what square is giving check? _____

108. Can Black block the check, move the King, or capture the attacker?

_____

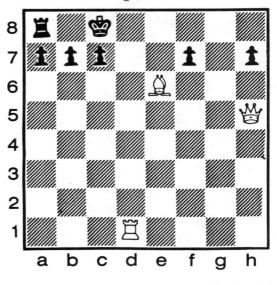

Diagram 130

109. In Diagram 131, which man of White's on what square is giving check? _____

110. Can Black block the check, move the King, or capture the attacker?

_____

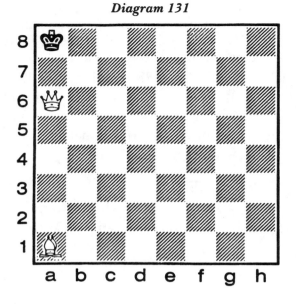

Diagram 131

111. In Diagram 132, which man of White's on what square is giving check? _____

112. Can Black block the check, move the King, or capture the attacker?

_____

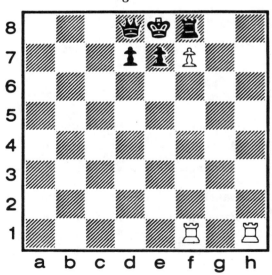

Diagram 132

113. In Diagram 133, which man on what square is giving check? _____

114. Can Black block the check, move the King, or capture the attacker?

_____

Diagram 133

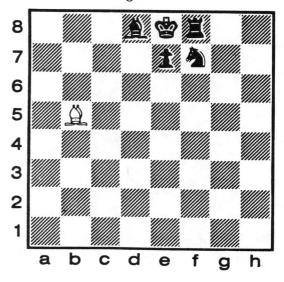

REVIEW OF CHECKS

Answer True or False.

115. An attack on the King is against the rules. _____

116. An attack on the King is a check.

_____

117. You can play any move you want when your King is in check.

_____

118. You must get your King out of check before you play any other move.

_____

119. You can get your King out of check only by capturing the attacker.

_____

120. You can get your King out of check only by moving it to a safe square.

_____

121. Only the White King can check the Black King. _____

122. Only a Queen can save a King.

_____

123. When the King is in check the game is over. _____

124. You can only check a King on a dark square. _____

Fill in the blank.

125. A _____ is an attack on the King.

126. You can get your King out of check in _____ different ways.

127. You can get your King out of check by _____ it to a safe square.

128. You can get your King out of check by moving another man between the _____ and the attacker.

129. You can get your King out of check by _____ the attacker.

130. If you cannot get your King out of _____ the game is over.

131. If your King is in check you _____ make any other move before you save it.

132. If your King is in check you must get it _____ of check or you have lost the game.

133. You may get your King out of _____ by blocking the attack.

134. You may _____ your King out of check by capturing the attacker.

Check your answers with those given in Answers for Chapter 4, pages 207–18.

CHAPTER 5

Checkmate

Checkmate is an attack on the King which cannot be stopped. When you checkmate the enemy King, you have won the game. If you are checkmated, you lose. Either way, the game is over.

We play chess with one main aim: to *checkmate* the enemy King. That is how a game of chess is won. In the end, it doesn't matter how many pieces or Pawns you have captured, or how long you have played. The only thing that counts is which King is checkmated.

Mate is a short word for checkmate. Checkmate and mate mean the same thing.

Look at Diagram 134. The White King is in big trouble.

1. Is White's King in check?

   _____

2. Name the piece or Pawn checking the White King and give the name of its square. _____

3. Can the White King move to a safe square? _____

4. Can the check to White's King be blocked? _____

5. Can the attacker of the White King be captured? _____

6. Is this checkmate for the White King?

   _____

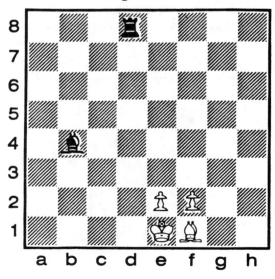

Diagram 134

Look at Diagrams 135 to 143 and see if White is checkmated. Remember to look for these things:

- *Black pieces or Pawns attacking White's King.*
- *A safe square for White's King.* If the King can escape to a safe square it is not mate.
- *A way to block Black's check to White's King.* If the check can be blocked it is not mate.
- *A way to capture Black's checking attackers.* If the checking attackers can be captured, it is not mate.

Diagram 135

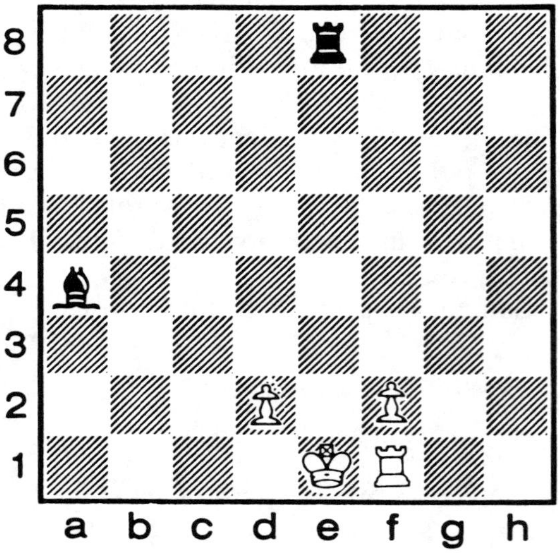

7. Name the man checking the White King in Diagram 135 _____
_____

8. Can White's King escape to a safe square? _____
_____

9. Can the check be blocked? _____
_____

10. Can the checking attacker be captured? _____
_____

11. Is it checkmate? _____
_____

12. Name the man checking the White King in Diagram 136: _____

_____

13. Can the White King escape to a safe square? _____

_____

14. Can the check be blocked? _____

_____

15. Can the checking attacker be captured? _____

_____

16. Is it checkmate? _____

_____

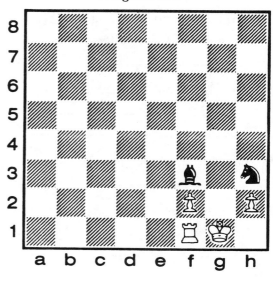

Diagram 136

17. Name the man checking the White King in Diagram 137: _____

_____

18. Can the White King escape to a safe square?_____

19. Can the check be blocked? _____

_____

20. Can the checking attacker be captured? _____

_____

21. Is it checkmate? _____

_____

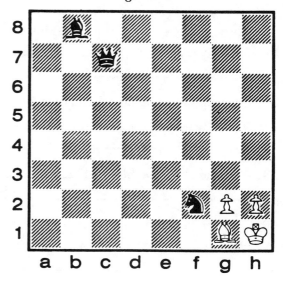

Diagram 137

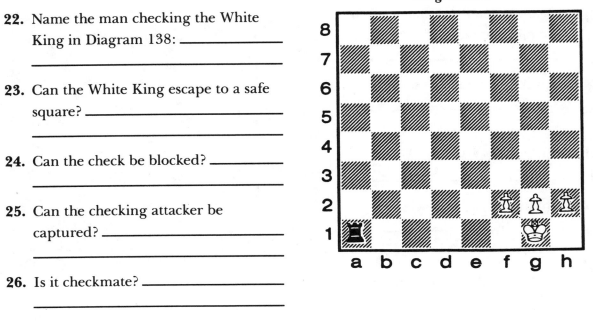

Diagram 138

22. Name the man checking the White King in Diagram 138: _____

_____

23. Can the White King escape to a safe square? _____

_____

24. Can the check be blocked? _____

_____

25. Can the checking attacker be captured? _____

_____

26. Is it checkmate? _____

_____

Diagram 139

27. Name the man checking the White King in Diagram 139: _____

_____

28. Can the White King escape to a safe square? _____

_____

29. Can the check be blocked? _____

_____

30. Can the checking attacker be captured? _____

_____

31. Is it checkmate? _____

_____

32. Name the man checking the White
King in Diagram 140: _____
_____

33. Can the White King escape to a safe
square? _____
_____

34. Can the check be blocked? _____
_____

35. Can the checking attacker be
captured? _____
_____

36. Is it checkmate? _____
_____

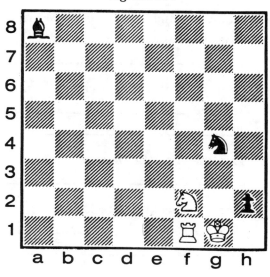

Diagram 140

37. Name the man checking the White
King in Diagram 141: _____
_____

38. Can the White King escape to a safe
square? _____
_____

39. Can the check be blocked? _____
_____

40. Can the checking attacker be
captured? _____
_____

41. Is it checkmate? _____

Diagram 141

Diagram 142

42. Name the man checking the White King in Diagram 142: _____

_____

43. Can the White King escape to a safe square? _____

_____

44. Can the check be blocked? _____

_____

45. Can the checking attacker be captured? _____

_____

46. Is it checkmate? _____

_____

Diagram 143

47. Name the man checking the White King in Diagram 143: _____

_____

48. Can the White King escape to a safe square? _____

_____

49. Can the check be blocked? _____

_____

50. Can the checking attacker be captured? _____

_____

51. Is it checkmate? _____

_____

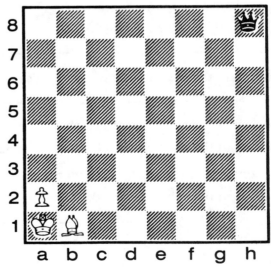

Goodie, goodie. You are White and you can checkmate the Black King on the next move. You win. All you have to do is find the right move. It is right there in Diagrams 144 to 153.

52. White's winning move in Diagram 144 is: _____

_____

Diagram 144

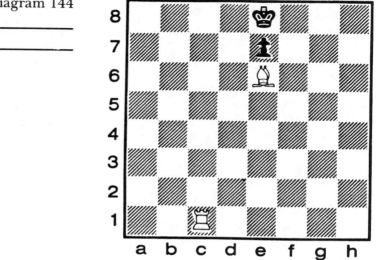

53. White's winning move in Diagram 145 is: _____

_____

Diagram 145

54. White's winning move in Diagram 146 is: _____

_____

Diagram 146

55. White's winning move in Diagram 147 is: _____

_____

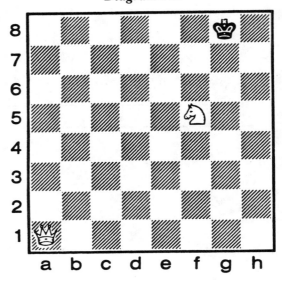

Diagram 147

56. White's winning move in Diagram 148 is: _____ _____

Diagram 148

57. White's winning move in Diagram 149 is: _____ _____

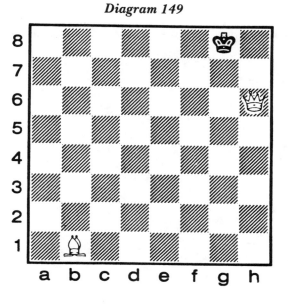

Diagram 149

58. White's winning move in Diagram 150
is: _____

_____

Diagram 150

59. White's winning move in Diagram 151
is: _____

_____

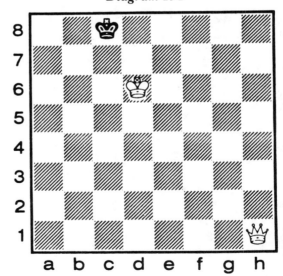

Diagram 151

60. White's winning move in Diagram 152 is: _____

_____

Diagram 152

61. White's winning move in Diagram 153 is: _____

_____

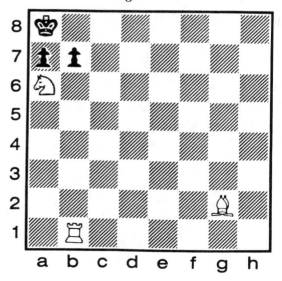

Diagram 153

Diagram 154 shows the most basic checkmate: a King and Queen together against a King by itself. Remember this pattern.

Diagram 154

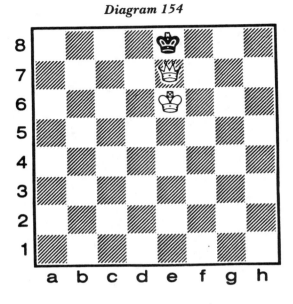

In Diagrams 155 to 159, you are playing with the Black pieces and have a really fine position on the chessboard. If you move the given piece or Pawn to the correct square, you can checkmate the White King.

62. In Diagram 155, move the Black
Bishop to: _____

_____

Diagram 155

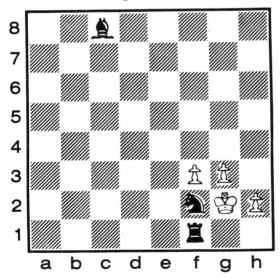

63. In Diagram 156, move the Black Knight to: _____

_____

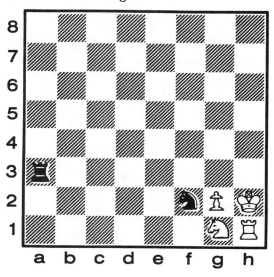

Diagram 156

64. In Diagram 157, move the Black Rook to: _____

_____

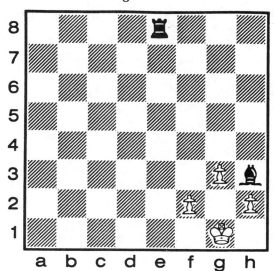

Diagram 157

65. In Diagram 158, move the Black
Queen to: _____

_____

Diagram 158

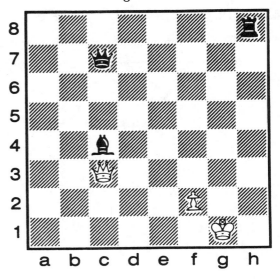

66. In Diagram 159, move the Black Pawn
to: _____

_____

Diagram 159

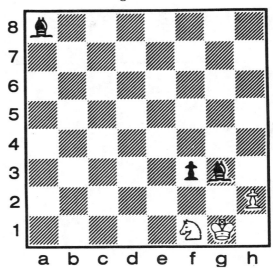

Diagram 160

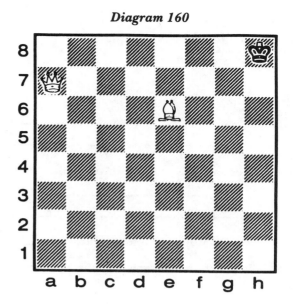

Oh, no! You weren't careful enough and you made a big mistake in Diagram 160. You were trying to checkmate the Black King and you *stalemated* it instead. It is Black's turn, but Black's only piece cannot move!

If the King is not directly under attack, but cannot move without moving into check, and no other Black piece or Pawn can be moved, then it is stalemate. In a stalemate, no one wins, but the game is over. A stalemate is a draw.

See how the Black King in Diagram 160 is unable to move. It cannot move anywhere without moving into check. *It is illegal for a King to move into check.* And Black has no other pieces or Pawns to move.

The game is over. White does not win. Black does not win. White does not lose. Black does not lose. We call this a *draw*. In a draw, nobody wins, and nobody loses. It's like a tie in sports.

White goes first. In most games, White begins the game on the offense and Black on the defense. In most games, Black would be happy to get a draw, but White would not. In every game, we should play to win.

In Diagrams 161 to 165, it is White's turn. For each example, you are to see if White is stalemated.

67. Is the White King in Diagram 161 under attack? _____

_____

68. Does the White King have a safe move? _____

_____

69. Does White have a legal move? _____

_____

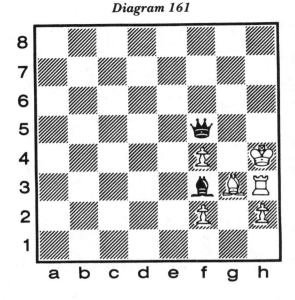

Diagram 161

70. Is the White King in Diagram 162 under attack? _____

_____

71. Does the White King have a safe move? _____

_____

72. Does White have a legal move? _____

_____

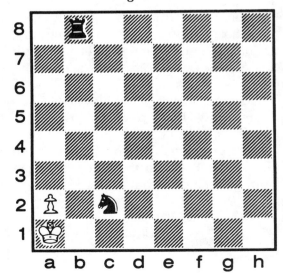

Diagram 162

73. Is the White King in Diagram 163 under attack? _____

_____

74. Does the White King have a safe move? _____

_____

75. Does White have a legal move? _____

_____

Diagram 163

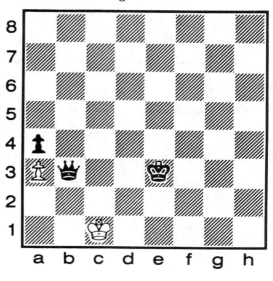

76. Is the White King in Diagram 164 under attack? _____

_____

77. Does the White King have a safe move? _____

_____

78. Does White have a legal move? _____

_____

Diagram 164

79. Is the White King in Diagram 165 under attack? _____

_____

80. Does the White King have a safe move? _____

_____

81. Does White have a legal move? _____

_____

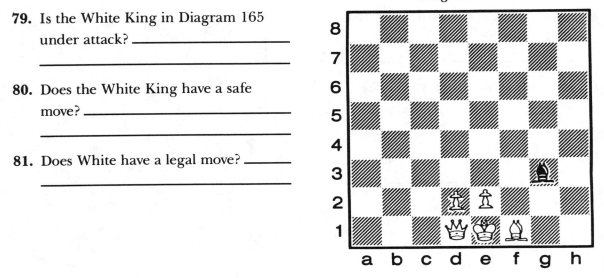

Diagram 165

How can you tell if it is stalemate or checkmate?

In stalemate, the King has no legal move but is not in check.

In checkmate, the King has no legal move but *is* in check.

In Diagrams 166 to 175, the Black King is either checkmated (you win) or stalemated (nobody wins). See if you can tell which is which. It is Black's turn in all examples.

82. In Diagram 166, does Black have any legal moves? _____

83. Is it check, checkmate, stalemate, or just Black's move? _____

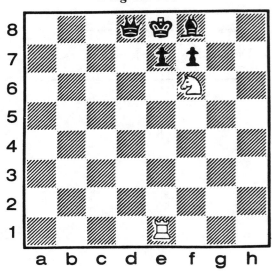

Diagram 166

84. In Diagram 167, does Black have any legal moves? _____

85. Is it check, checkmate, stalemate, or just Black's move? _____

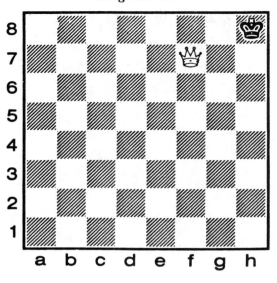

Diagram 167

86. In Diagram 168, does Black have any legal moves? _____

87. Is it check, checkmate, stalemate, or just Black's move? _____ .

Diagram 168

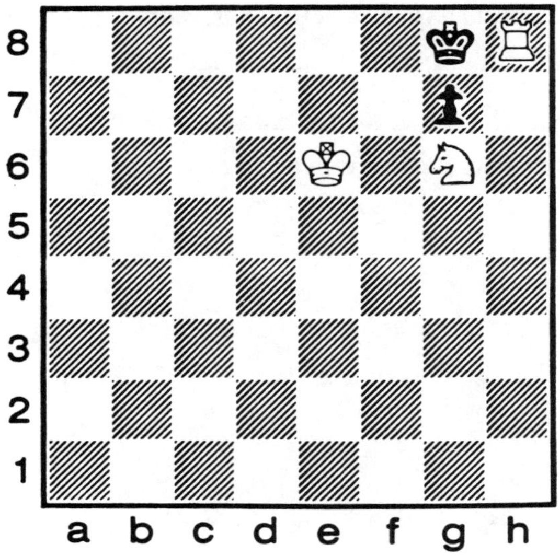

88. In Diagram 169, does Black have any legal moves? _____

89. Is it check, checkmate, stalemate, or just Black's move? _____

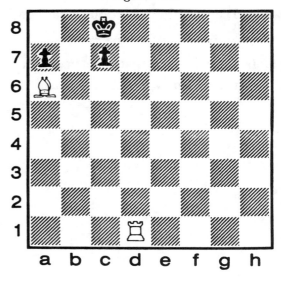

Diagram 169

90. In Diagram 170, does Black have any legal moves? _____

91. Is it check, checkmate, stalemate, or just Black's move? _____

Diagram 170

92. In Diagram 171, does Black have any legal moves? _____

93. Is it check, checkmate, stalemate, or just Black's move? _____

Diagram 171

94. In Diagram 172, does Black have any legal moves? _____

95. Is it check, checkmate, stalemate, or just Black's move? _____

Diagram 172

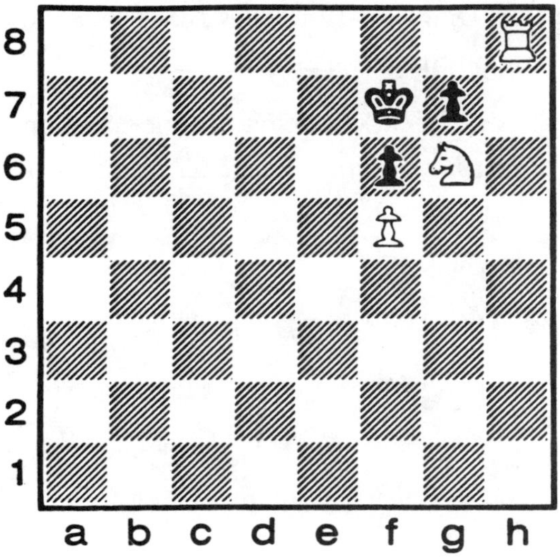

96. In Diagram 173, does Black have any legal moves? _____

97. Is it check, checkmate, stalemate, or just Black's move? _____

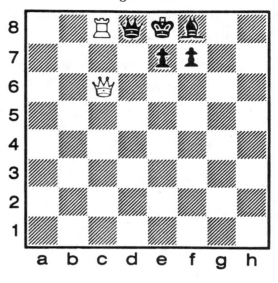

Diagram 173

98. In Diagram 174, does Black have any legal moves? _____

99. Is it check, checkmate, stalemate, or just Black's move? _____

Diagram 174

100. In Diagram 175, does Black have any legal moves? _____

101. Is it check, checkmate, stalemate, or just Black's move? _____

Diagram 175

REVIEW OF CHECKMATE AND STALEMATE

Fill in the blanks.

102. _____ is an attack on the King which cannot be stopped.

103. The game of chess is won by mating the enemy _____.

104. It is _____ when the King in check has no safe square.

105. Mate is an attack which cannot be _____.

106. Checkmate means _____.

107. If the King is not in check and neither the King nor any of his comrades have a legal move, it is _____.

108. In stalemate, no one _____ and no one _____.

109. Stalemate is also called a _____.

110. A draw is a _____.

111. If the King is _____ it is under attack; if it is _____ it is not under attack.

112. If you checkmate the enemy King you _____ the game.

113. If you stalemate the enemy King you do not _____ the game.

Check your answers against those given in Answers for Chapter 5, pages 219–26.

CHAPTER 6

Special Moves: Queening and Castling

In chess there are several special moves. Two of them are *Queening* and *castling*. We talked briefly about Queening in Chapter 1. Now we will talk about it again.

Another name for Queening is promotion. Diagram 176 shows a White Pawn on b7, ready to Queen. Diagram 177 shows it reaching the last rank, and Diagram 178 shows White promoting the Pawn to a Queen. That's Pawn magic.

Remember these things about Pawns:

- *Pawns can only move forward.* They can never go backward.
- *Pawns can move forward only one square at a time,* except on their first move, when they can move two squares.
- *Pawns are the lowliest of all the chessmen.* They are worth only 1 point.

Diagram 176

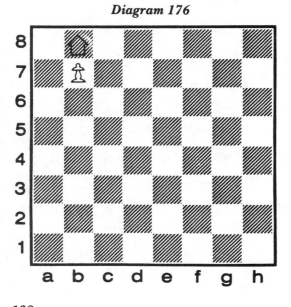

Diagram 177

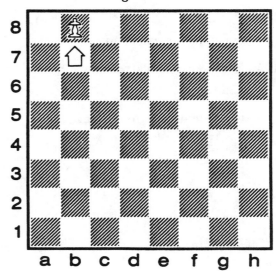

Now here is something new: When a Pawn reaches the last rank on the side of the chessboard opposite the side where it started, it can become any piece you want except a King or Pawn. It can become a Queen, Rook, Bishop, or Knight.

You can make a new Queen, even if you still have your original Queen on the board. You can do better than that, too! If somehow all eight of your Pawns reach the last rank, you could change all of them into Queens, though one extra Queen is usually enough to win.

Just imagine it! When the chess fairy tale was over, you could have as many as nine Queens: the one you started with and the eight new ones you made.

If you wanted, you could also have ten Knights: the two you started with and eight new ones. Or ten Rooks (the starting two plus eight new ones), or five Queens (one old and four new) and six Rooks (two old and four new), or any combination that adds up to eight new pieces. But you usually don't need that many to win. Most of the time, making one new Queen by promoting a Pawn is enough to give you a winning advantage.

That's Pawn magic. We call it Queening, since nearly all the time a player will change the promoted Pawn into a new Queen, because the Queen is the most powerful and valuable piece. Then the Pawn changes from the weakest chessman to the strongest.

Look back at Diagrams 176 to 178. What would happen if the Pawn on b7 in Diagram 176 moved to b8, as in Diagram 177, and suddenly became a Queen, as in Diagram 178?

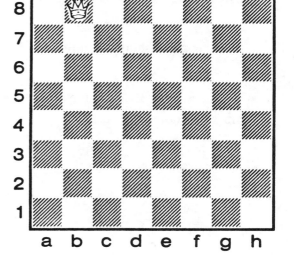

Diagram 178

1. Would White's new Queen be able to do all the things an ordinary Queen does? Would it be able to move and capture like a regular Queen?

   _____

2. Would the new White Queen be able to give check, as an ordinary Queen could? _____

3. Would the new Queen be able to mate, as an ordinary Queen could?

   _____

In Diagrams 179 to 184, there is a White Pawn that is about to promote. Answer these questions about the promoting Pawn.

4. In Diagram 179, what square does the White Pawn sit on before promoting?

_____

5. If the Pawn moves to the last rank, what pieces can the Pawn become?

_____

6. Are you allowed to have two Queens on the board at the same time?

_____

7. Once the Pawn promotes to a new Queen, it would be checking Black's King. How does Black get out of check? _____

8. Instead of making a Queen, what other piece could White make and still give mate? _____

9. In Diagram 180, what is the name of the promotion square? _____

10. What new piece should White make?

_____

11. What move must Black make after White's promotion? _____

12. What other new piece would be just as good as a Queen here? _____

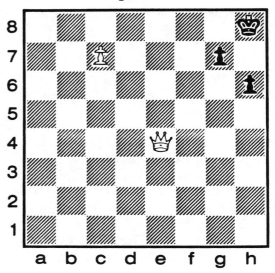

Diagram 179

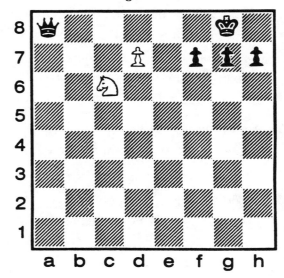

Diagram 180

13. In Diagram 181, what is the name of the promotion square? _____

14. What new piece should White make? _____

15. What move must Black play after White promotes? _____

Diagram 181

16. In Diagram 182, what is the name of the promotion square? _____

17. What new piece should White make? _____

Diagram 182

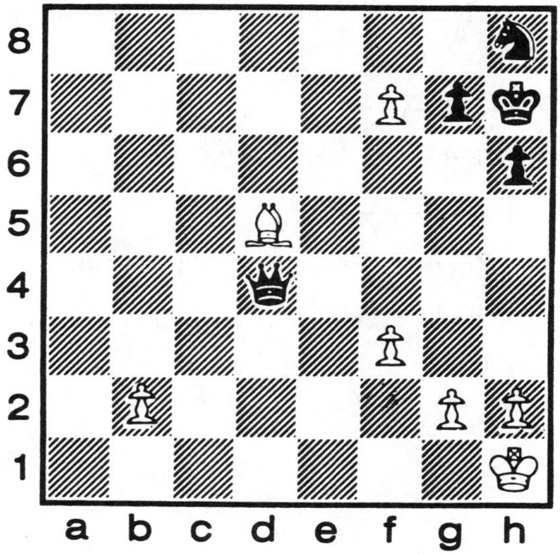

18. In Diagram 183, what is the name of the promotion square? _____

19. What new piece should White make? _____

20. What's wrong with making a new Queen? _____

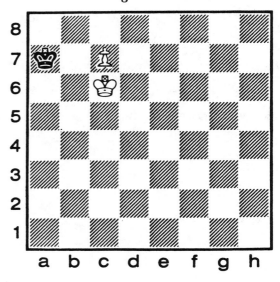

Diagram 183

21. In Diagram 184, what are the names of White's promotion squares? _____

22. What new piece should White make? _____

23. Which of the three Pawn promotions is best? _____

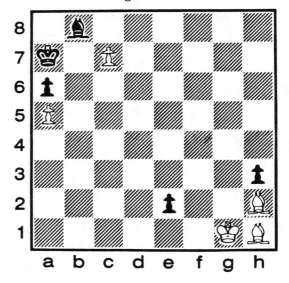

Diagram 184

In Diagrams 185 to 187, it is Black's turn to promote a Pawn. In Diagram 185, the Black Pawn is on f2. In Diagram 186, it moves to f1. In Diagram 187, the Pawn is promoted to a Queen, and the White King is checkmated.

Diagram 185

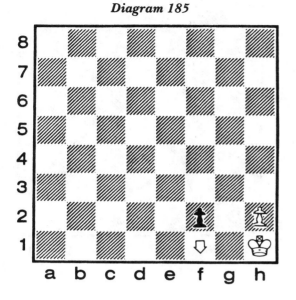

Diagram 186

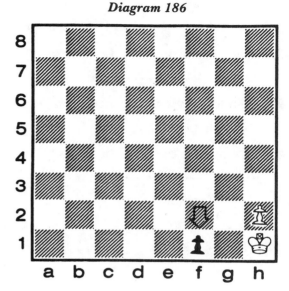

Diagram 187

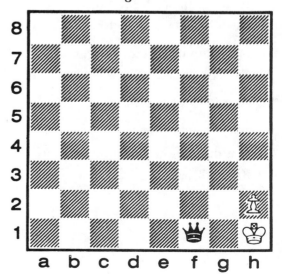

In Diagrams 188 to 192, see if the Black Pawn should become a Queen or a Knight.

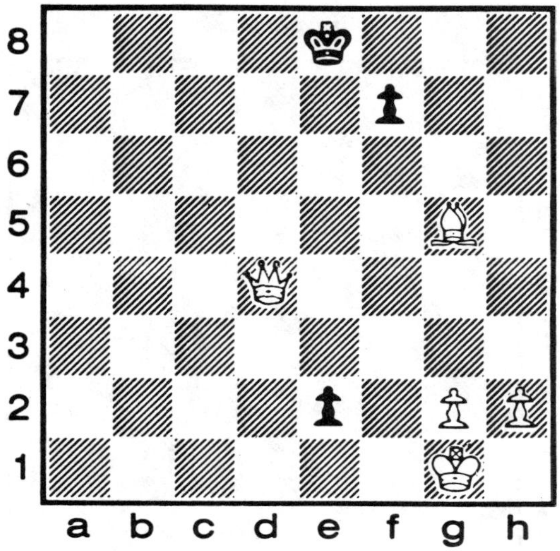

24. In Diagram 188, should the Black Pawn become a Queen? _____

25. Is it mate if the Pawn becomes a Queen? _____

26. Should the Pawn become a Knight? _____

27. Is it mate if the Pawn becomes a Knight? _____

Diagram 188

28. In Diagram 189, should the Black Pawn become a Queen? _____

29. Is it mate if the Pawn becomes a Queen? _____

30. Should the Pawn become a Knight? _____

31. Is it mate if the Pawn becomes a Knight? _____

Diagram 189

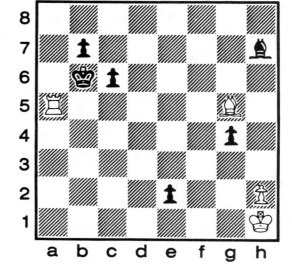

32. In Diagram 190, should the Black Pawn become a Queen? _____

33. Is it mate if the Pawn becomes a Queen? _____

34. Should the Pawn become a Knight? _____

35. Is it mate if the Pawn becomes a Knight? _____

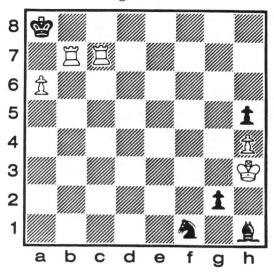

Diagram 190

36. In Diagram 191, should the Black Pawn become a Queen? _____

37. Is it mate if the Pawn becomes a Queen? _____

38. Should the Pawn become a Knight? _____

39. Is it mate if the Pawn becomes a Knight? _____

Diagram 191

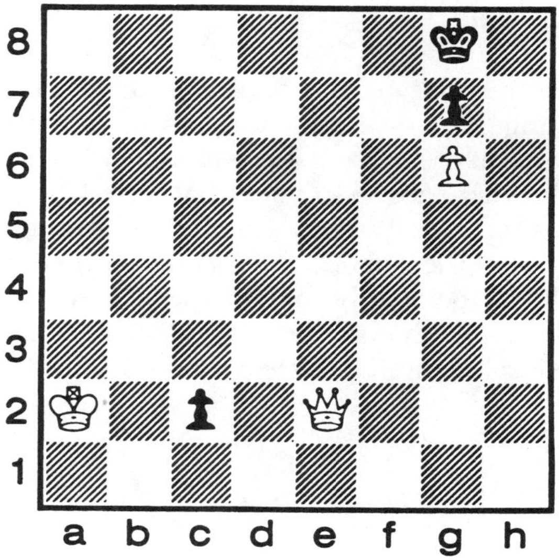

40. In Diagram 192, should the Black Pawn become a Queen? _____

41. Is it mate if the Pawn becomes a Queen? _____

42. Should the Pawn become a Knight? _____

43. Is it mate if the Pawn becomes a Knight? _____

Diagram 192

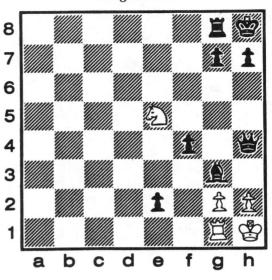

Castling

Pawns can Queen, and Kings can castle. In all good fairy tales, the King has a safe home to go to when the armies are battling. It's the same in chess. Each side is allowed to castle once during a chess game. But there are strict rules that limit when castling is legally possible.

Once the Pawns in front of the Kings have been moved, after the start of the game, the Kings may be in danger. They have no walls to shield them. It becomes easier for enemy men to attack them. Diagram 193 shows a position before the White King has castled. Black's King has already castled on the Kingside of the board.

Look at Diagram 193 carefully and think about the questions below:

Diagram 193

44. On which square is the White King? Is it the square on which the King began the game? _____

45. Are there any Pawns in front of the White King, blocking the open files and offering shelter for the King?

_____

46. Is Black waiting for a chance to check the White King along the e-file? _____

_____

47. Where are White's Rooks? _____

48. On which square is the Black King? Is it the square on which the King began the game? _____

49. Are there any Pawns in front of the Black King, blocking the open files and defending the King? _____

50. Is the White Rook or any White piece or Pawn able to check the Black King on the next move? _____

51. Where are Black's Rooks? _____

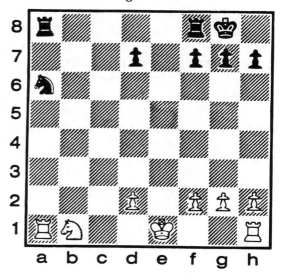

When the King castles, it is the only time in the chess game that two pieces can be moved together on the same turn.

It is also the only time in a chess game that the King can move more than one square at a time.

It is also the only time a Rook can jump over another piece.

White castles Kingside by moving the King two squares toward the Rook on h1. This means the King lands on g1. Then the Kingside Rook is moved from h1 to the other side of the King. This means the Rook lands on f1. This is *castling Kingside.*

Even though two pieces are shifted, the whole play is considered one move. Diagrams 194 to 196 show Kingside castling for White, before, during, and after the move is played.

The White King can *castle Queenside,* too. It is done the same way as castling Kingside, but on the Queenside of the board. First, the King moves two squares toward the Rook at a1. This means the King lands on c1. Then the Queenside Rook moves to the other side of the King. This means the Rook lands on d1, the starting square for White's Queen. Diagrams 197 and 198 show how White castles Queenside.

Diagram 194

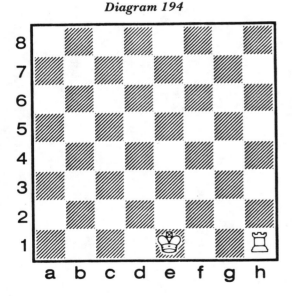

Diagram 195

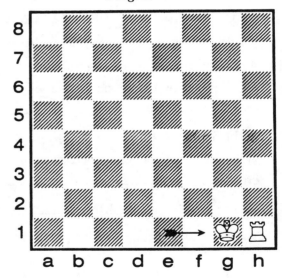

Diagram 196

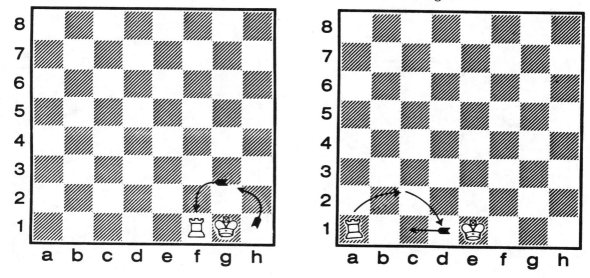

Diagram 197

Diagram 198

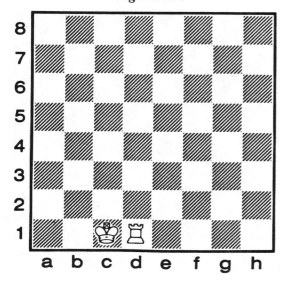

Black is allowed to castle once during a chess game, too. If it is possible, Black may castle Kingside or Queenside. For Kingside castling, Black's King moves to g8 and the Rook on h8 goes to f8. Diagrams 199 and 200 show how Black Castles Kingside.

For Queenside castling, Black's King stops on c8 and his Rook on a8 goes to d8. Diagrams 201 and 202 show how Black castles Queenside.

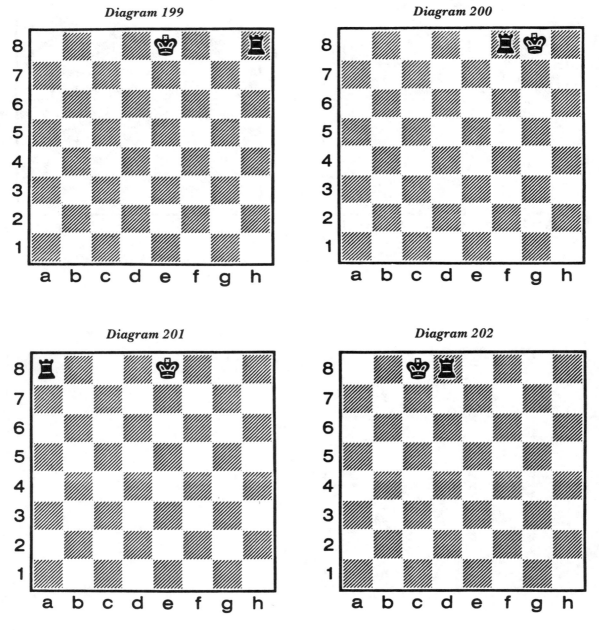

Diagram 199

Diagram 200

Diagram 201

Diagram 202

In Diagram 203, White wants to castle. Some things could stop White from castling, though. They are:

Diagram 203

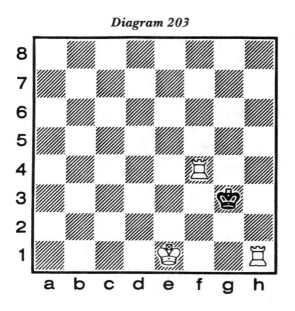

- *Being in check stops you from castling.* You *cannot* castle if you are in check. You must get out of check first, then you may be able to castle.
- *You cannot castle through check.* In other words, when castling, the King *cannot* pass over a square guarded by the enemy. If a piece is attacking a square between the King and the Rook, the King *cannot* castle. Drive the enemy piece away and you may be able to castle.
- *You cannot castle into check.* The King can *never* move into check.
- *You cannot castle if there are pieces between the King and the Rook.* There must be only empty squares between the King and the Rook to castle. The Bishop and Knight that begin the game on these squares must be moved out of the way before you can castle.
- *The King and the Rook to be castled must not have been moved.* If neither the King nor the Rook has been moved off the squares where they began the chess game, you may be able to castle. If either the King or the Rook to be castled has been moved even once, you cannot castle. Even if you move the King and its castling Rook back to their original squares, you're no longer allowed to castle.

The squares on which the King and Rooks start the game are

e1 for White's King and
e8 for Black's King,
a1 for White's Queenside Rook and
h1 for White's Kingside Rook, and
a8 for Black's Queenside Rook and
h8 for Black's Kingside Rook.

You have the White pieces. Your King is out in the open. Black wants to attack it. What can you do?

In Diagrams 204 to 206, you'd like to castle. See if you are able to castle Kingside, Queenside, both, or neither.

Look for these things first:

- Are you in check?
- Would you have to castle through check?
- Would you be castling into check?
- Are there any pieces in the way?
- Are the King and Rook on their original squares? (In the diagrams below, if King and Rook are on their original squares, it means they have not moved before and then moved back.)

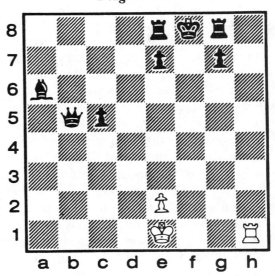

Diagram 204

52. In Diagram 204, is White in check?

_____

53. Would White have to castle through check? _____

54. Would White be castling into check?

_____

55. Are there any pieces in the way?

_____

56. Are the King and Rook on their original squares? _____

57. Can White castle? _____

58. In Diagram 205, is White in check?
_____

59. Would White have to castle through check? _____

60. Would White be castling into check?
_____

61. Are there any pieces in the way?
_____

62. Are the King and Rook on their original squares? _____

63. Can White castle? _____

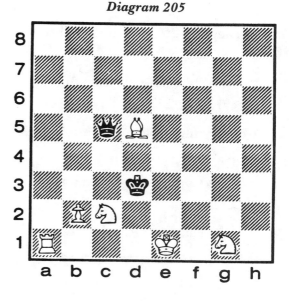

Diagram 205

64. In Diagram 206, is White in check?
_____

65. Would White have to castle through check? _____

66. Would White be castling into check?
_____

67. Are there any pieces in the way?
_____

68. Are the King and Rook on their original squares? _____

69. Can White castle? _____

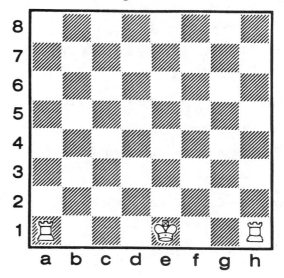

Diagram 206

70. In Diagram 207, is White in check?
_____

71. Would White have to castle through check? _____

72. Would White be castling into check? _____

73. Are there any pieces in the way? _____

74. Are the King and Rook on their original squares? _____

75. Can White castle? _____

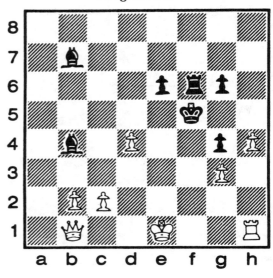

Diagram 207

76. In Diagram 208, is White in check? _____

77. Would White have to castle through check? _____

78. Would White be castling into check? _____

79. Are there any pieces in the way? _____

80. Are the King and Rook on their original squares? _____

81. Can White castle? _____

Diagram 208

82. In Diagram 209, is White in check?

_____

83. Would White have to castle through check? _____

84. Would White be castling into check?

_____

85. Are there any pieces in the way?

_____

86. Are the King and Rook on their original squares? _____

87. Can White castle? _____

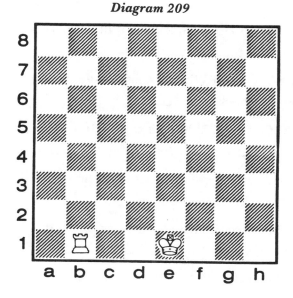

Diagram 209

88. In Diagram 210, is White in check?

_____

89. Would White have to castle through check? _____

90. Would White be castling into check?

_____

91. Are there any pieces in the way?

_____

92. Are the King and Rook on their original squares? _____

93. Can White castle? _____

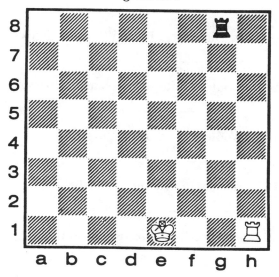

Diagram 210

94. In Diagram 211, is White in check?

_____

95. Would White have to castle through check? _____

96. Would White be castling into check?

_____

97. Are there any pieces in the way?

_____

98. Are the King and Rook on their original squares? _____

99. Can White castle? _____

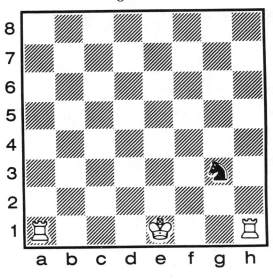

Diagram 211

100. In Diagram 212, is White in check?

_____

101. Would White have to castle through check? _____

102. Would White be castling into check?

_____

103. Are there any pieces in the way?

_____

104. Are the King and Rook on their original squares? _____

105. Can White castle? _____

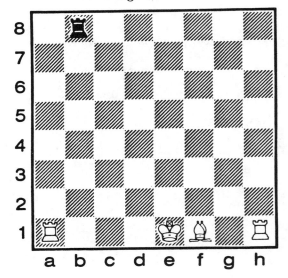

Diagram 212

REVIEWING QUEENING AND CASTLING

Answer True or False.

106. In Pawn magic, the Queening Pawn can change into any piece except a Queen. _____

107. A Pawn Queens when it reaches the last rank on the side of the chessboard opposite where it started. _____

108. You can Queen a Pawn only if you no longer have your original Queen. _____

109. When you Queen a Pawn, you must make a new Queen. _____

110. A promoted piece has the same abilities as an original piece. _____

111. You cannot promote while making a capture. _____

112. A promoted Queen is worth 8 points. _____

113. You can promote a Pawn and checkmate with the same move. _____

114. If the enemy King is castled, you can promote a Pawn by reaching the 7th rank. _____

115. Though you are allowed to make pieces other than a Queen, it is always better to promote a Pawn to a new Queen. _____

Fill in the Blanks.

116. Pawns may Queen and Kings may _____.

117. A King can never castle into _____.

118. A King can never castle out of _____.

119. The only time a King can move more than one square on a turn is when it _____.

120. The only time a Rook can jump over another piece is when the King _____.

121. When it castles, the King moves _____ squares toward the Rook.

122. A King can castle Kingside or _____.

123. You cannot castle if the King has been _____ before.

124. You cannot castle if the Rook has been _____ before.

Go to the answer section and see how you did.

Check your answers against those given in Answers to Chapter 6, pages 227–36.

CHAPTER 7

Draws

When you play a game of chess, if you are the better player you should win. If you make a mistake you might lose. But if both chess players are equal, there is a good chance that the game will be a draw.

When a game is a draw, no one wins and no one loses.

In Chapter 5, on checkmates, we learned one way that a chess game might be drawn—by *stalemate*. When the King is not in check but has no legal moves to make, and none of the King's men have any legal moves to make either, then it is stalemate.

How to Draw a Chessgame #1

A stalemate is a draw.

In diagrams 213 to 217, the game is drawn if Black is in stalemate. But maybe it's not stalemate. Perhaps White can still win. See if you can tell which examples are drawn and which are not. In all cases, it is Black's turn to play.

1. Is Diagram 213 a stalemate?

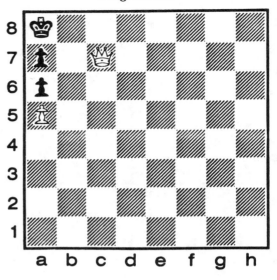

Diagram 213

2. Is Diagram 214 a stalemate?

Diagram 214

3. Is Diagram 215 a stalemate?

_____

Diagram 215

4. Is Diagram 216 a stalemate?

_____

Diagram 216

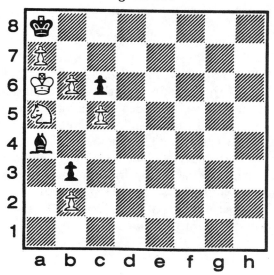

5. Is Diagram 217 a stalemate?

_____

Diagram 217

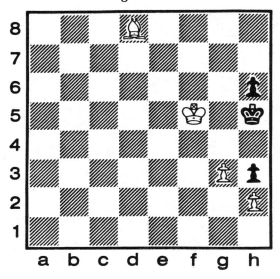

How to Draw a Chessgame #2:

It is a draw if both players say it is a draw. They can agree to a draw.

This happens very often. After playing a long game and having lots of fun, sometimes both players will decide neither of them has a real chance to win. Both players might see that they could easily lose, too, especially by mistake. Then one of the players will ask the other if they wish to call it a draw.

If both players agree that the game is a draw, that neither player has a good chance to win, then the game is over. No one wins, no one loses. Diagrams 218 to 221 show four examples of positions in which the players might agree to a draw. In these diagrams, neither player has good winning chances.

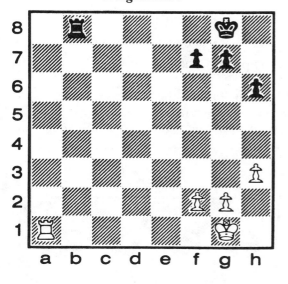

Diagram 218

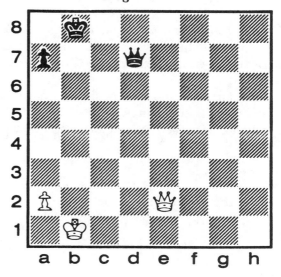

Diagram 219

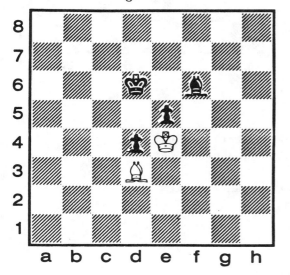

Diagram 220

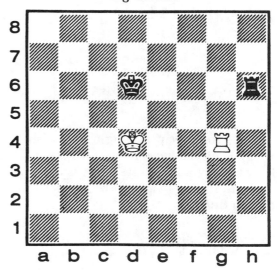

Diagram 221

How to Draw a Chessgame #3:

It is a draw if no one has enough men to checkmate the enemy King.

If you have taken every one of the enemy men except the King and all of your own men except the King have also been captured, then it is a draw.

Diagram 222 shows a position where the only men left on the board are the two Kings. White has taken all of Black's other men, and Black has taken every Pawn and every piece that White has, too.

Diagram 222

6. Can the White King on e4 get any closer to the Black King on e6?

_____

7. Can a King ever move into check?

_____

8. Can a King ever move more than one square at a time? _____

9. Can one King ever checkmate another? _____

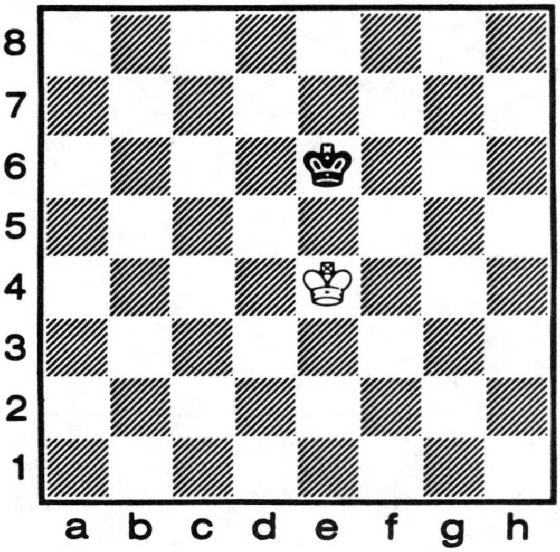

In the same way, a King and a Bishop can never checkmate the enemy King. If one side has only a King and a Bishop, and the other side has only a King, the game is a draw.

Diagrams 223 to 230 show positions with few chessmen left. See if you can find out

- whether White can ever checkmate Black or
- whether Black can ever checkmate White, or
- whether the game is drawn because neither side has enough men to checkmate the other.

10. In Diagram 223, can White ever checkmate Black? _____

11. Can Black ever checkmate White? _____

12. Is it a draw? _____

Diagram 223

13. In Diagram 224, can White ever checkmate Black? _____

14. Can Black ever checkmate White? _____

15. Is it a draw? _____

Diagram 224

16. In Diagram 225, can White ever checkmate Black? _____

17. Can Black ever checkmate White? _____

18. Is it a draw? _____

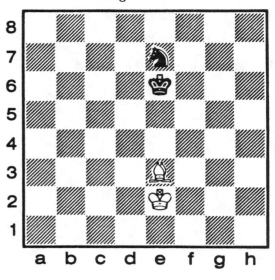

Diagram 225

19. In Diagram 226, can White ever checkmate Black? _____

20. Can Black ever checkmate White? _____

21. Is it a draw? _____

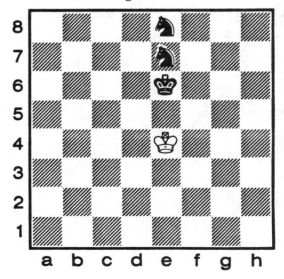

Diagram 226

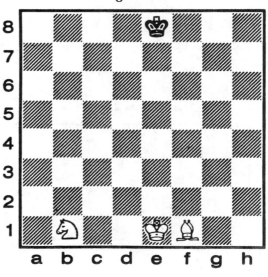

Diagram 227

22. In Diagram 227, can White ever checkmate Black? _____

23. Can Black ever checkmate White? _____

24. Is it a draw? _____

Diagrams 228 to 231 show why two Knights cannot force checkmate.

In Diagram 228, White's King on b6 and Knight on d6 trap Black's King in the corner. Black's King can move between b8 and a8, back and forth.

Diagram 228

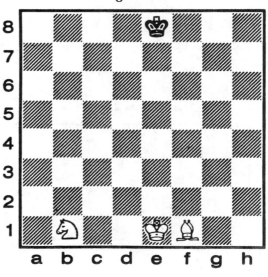

In Diagram 229, White's other Knight gives check, moving from a5 to c6.

In Diagram 230, Black's King moves to its only safe square, a8 in the corner. The King can't move to c8 because the Knight on d6 guards c8.

Diagram 229

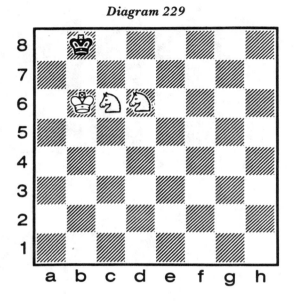

Diagram 230

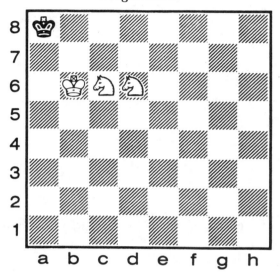

In Diagram 231, the White Knight moves from d6 to b5 (it could also move to c7 by first moving to e8). White wants to checkmate Black at c7 on the next move. But White has not looked at the position very carefully, because after the Knight goes from d6 to b5, Black doesn't have a legal move. Stalemate.

The game is drawn. White cannot force a winning game. One move before checkmate, White forces stalemate. The game is over.

Diagram 231

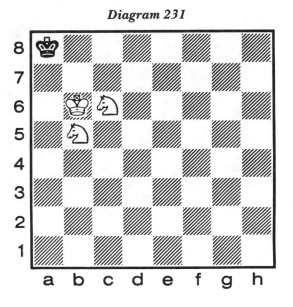

How to Draw a Chessgame #4:

If the exact same position is reached three times in one chess game, a draw can be claimed.

This rule is also called the *threefold repetition rule*. The exact same positions do not have to happen three times in a row. The same player must be on move, though.

Let's say that a position happens the first time. Then, four moves later, it happens again. If the very same position is about to happen a third time, even 20 moves later, the player who is about to move (and who in doing so will create the position that has already occurred twice) can claim a draw.

Of course, if the same position happens three times in a row, it's easier to spot. One reason to write down your moves is to spot the threefold repetition. You can always check the moves to see what happened, rather than trying to remember everything in your head.

A chess game is being played in Diagrams 232 to 243. Look at each diagram carefully and answer the questions to see if Black can claim a draw by the threefold repetition rule.

25. In Diagram 232, it is White's turn to move. Name the squares on which the White pieces sit. _____

26. Name the squares on which the Black pieces sit. _____

27. How many times has this position occurred so far? _____

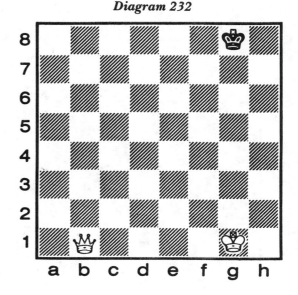

Diagram 232

28. In Diagram 233, what move has White played? _____

29. How many times has this position occurred? _____

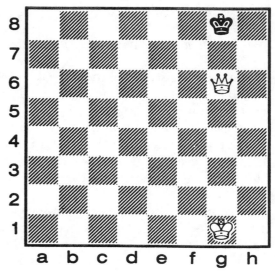

Diagram 233

30. In Diagram 234, what move has Black
played? _____

31. How many times has this position
occurred? _____

Diagram 234

32. In Diagram 235, what move has
White played? _____

33. How many times has this position
occurred? _____

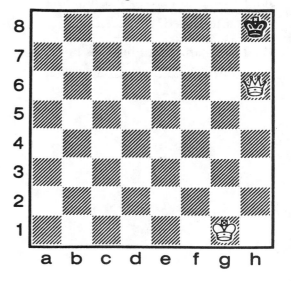

Diagram 235

34. In Diagram 236, what move has Black played? _____

35. How many times has this position occurred? _____

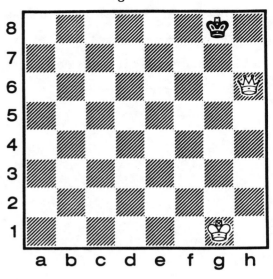

Diagram 236

36. In Diagram 237, what move has White played? _____

37. How many times has this position occurred? _____

Diagram 237

38. In Diagram 238, what move has Black played? _____

39. How many times has this position occurred? _____

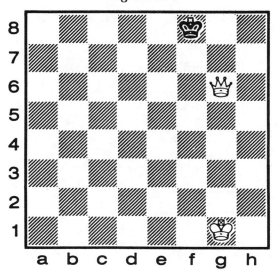

Diagram 238

40. In Diagram 239, what move has White played? _____

41. How many times has this position occurred? _____

42. Can Black claim a draw?

_____

43. Can White claim a draw?

_____

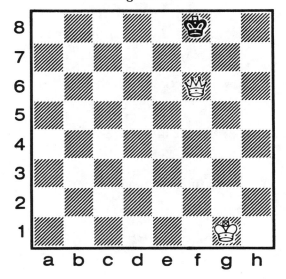

Diagram 239

44. In Diagram 240, what move has Black played? _____

45. How many times has this position occurred? _____

46. Can Black claim a draw? _____

47. Can White claim a draw? _____

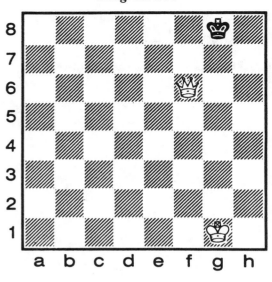

Diagram 240

48. In Diagram 241, what move has White played? _____

49. How many times has this position occurred? _____

50. Can Black claim a draw? _____

51. Can White claim a draw? _____

Diagram 241

52. In Diagram 242, what move has Black played? _____

53. How many times has this position occurred? _____

54. Can Black claim a draw? _____

55. Can White claim a draw? _____

56. In which three diagrams above was the exact position repeated? _____

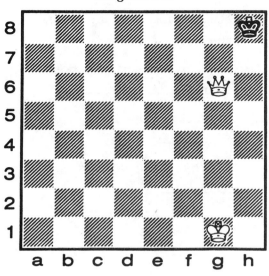

Diagram 242

57. In Diagram 243, what move has White played? _____

58. How many times has this position occurred? _____

59. Can Black claim a draw? _____

60. Can White claim a draw? _____

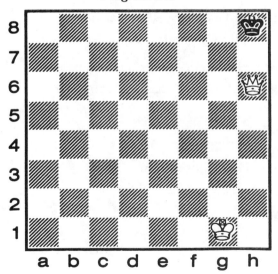

Diagram 243

61. In Diagram 244, what move has Black
played? _____

62. How many times has this position
occurred? _____

63. Can Black claim a draw?
_____

64. Can White claim a draw?
_____

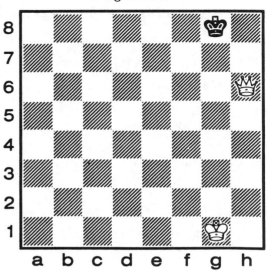

Diagram 244

65. In Diagram 245, what move has
White played? _____

66. How many times has this position
occurred? _____

67. Can Black claim a draw?
_____

68. Can White claim a draw?
_____

Diagram 245

Diagram 246

69. Diagram 246 shows what the position will be if Black now moves to h8. In which two other diagrams has this position occurred before?

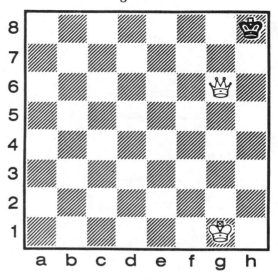

_____

How to Draw a Chess Game #5:

If 50 moves have been played without a man being captured or a Pawn moved, the player whose turn it is can claim a draw.

The draw is usually claimed by the player with the worst of it on that player's turn. If you have extra men and a winning game, you want to avoid the 50-move rule. You want to mate before 50 moves (that's 50 for White and 50 for Black) have been played.

If you have a winning game, but find that your opponent is counting moves and hoping for a draw, you may be able to get more time. All you have to do is push a Pawn. As soon as you move a Pawn, the counting must start all over again. Then you have another 50 moves.

If for some reason you can't move a Pawn, then you can make a capture. That, too, gives you 50 more moves. You can even wait to move 49 and then make an exchange or move a Pawn, and the count must start over.

This is another reason we must learn to write down the moves of our chess games. You cannot claim a draw or stop someone from claiming one by the 50-move rule if you don't remember what the moves were.

Most of the time, the stronger side doesn't need 50 moves to win, so the rule is almost never used. But once in a rare while, the rule may help you save a game—if you know about it.

REVIEW OF DRAWS

Fill in the blanks.

70. In chess, you can win a game, you can lose a game, and you can _____ a game.

71. When you draw a chess game, no one _____ and no one _____.

72. A stalemate is a _____.

73. It is stalemate when the King has no _____ moves to make and neither do any of the King's men.

74. It is a draw if both _____ say it is a draw.

In the answer section, there are more answers than diagrams. This is because some of the diagrams have more than one chess puzzle hidden in them. For answers without diagrams, see the question diagram of the same number.

Answers for Chapter 1

1. There are eight squares in each row that go across the chessboard. The first square on the bottom left-hand corner is dark, the second is light, the third is dark, and so on. The dark and light squares alternate across the board.

2. There are eight squares in each row that goes from the bottom to the top of the chessboard. The first square in the bottom left-hand corner, as we know, is dark. The square just above it is light. The third square from the bottom is dark again. The dark and light squares alternate up and down the board, too.

3. Every chessboard has 64 squares in a pattern of alternating light and dark colors. Checkerboards have the same number of squares laid out in the same way. In fact, a chessboard is a checkerboard.

   We could learn how many squares a chessboard has by counting each square, or by using multiplication. A chessboard has 64 squares altogether, that is,

       8 rows of squares across
   × 8 rows of squares up and down
     64 squares altogether

4. A chessboard has 32 dark squares. Since every other square is a dark square, half the total number of squares are dark. We could count the number of dark squares on a chessboard, or we could use division to find out how many there are.

   $$64 \div 2 = 32$$

5. A chessboard has 32 light squares. If there are 32 dark squares, there must also be 32 light squares. The number of dark and light squares on a chessboard is even.

       32 light squares
   + 32 dark squares
       64 squares altogether

6. The longest light diagonal, which has eight squares, is shown in Answer Diagram 1. It starts on White's right-hand side, on the square named h1, and goes from that bottom corner to the top left-hand corner at a8. The longest light diagonal is called the a8–h1 diagonal.

There is also a longest dark diagonal. It has eight squares, too. The longest dark diagonal starts on the square named a1 in the left-hand corner, and goes from the bottom to the top right-hand corner at h8. It is called the a1–h8 diagonal.

Answer Diagram 1

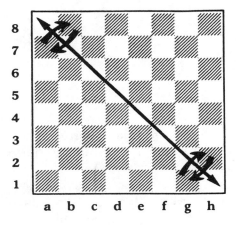

7. The shortest dark diagonals have two squares each. One is in the bottom right-hand corner on White's side. It goes from the square named g1 to the square named h2. It is called the g1–h2 diagonal.

The other is at the top on the left side of the board. It goes from the square named a7 to the square named b8. It is called the a7–b8 diagonal.

There are short light diagonals, too. One is in the bottom corner on White's left-hand side. It goes from the square named a2 to the square named b1. It is called the a2–b1 diagonal. The other is in the top right-hand corner. It goes from the square named g8 to the square named h7. It is called the g8–h7 diagonal.

The diagonals take their names from the names of the squares where they begin and end, with the lower letter in the alphabet named first.

8. There are 16 pieces in the White and Black armies combined. White has eight pieces, and so does Black. Rooks, Knights, Bishops, Queen, and King are pieces. Black has two Rooks, two Knights, two Bishops, one Queen, and one King. White has the same. Remember, Pawns are not pieces.

$$\begin{array}{r} 8 \text{ White pieces} \\ + \underline{\ 8 \text{ Black pieces}} \\ 16 \text{ pieces combined} \end{array}$$

9. There are 16 Pawns in the White and Black armies combined.

$$\begin{array}{r} 8 \text{ White Pawns} \\ + \underline{\ 8 \text{ Black Pawns}} \\ 16 \text{ Pawns combined} \end{array}$$

10. There are 32 men in both armies. A chessman is either a Pawn or a piece. Even the Queen is called a chessman.

Usually, we call chessmen "men" for short.

$$\begin{array}{r} 16 \text{ pieces combined} \\ + \underline{16 \text{ Pawns combined}} \\ 32 \text{ men in both armies} \end{array}$$

11. Pawns can move either one or two squares on their first move. In Answer Diagram 5, the marked squares show where the Pawns could move on their first moves. The squares where the Pawns could move are named by combining the letter of the file with the number of the rank. More on this later.

The White Pawn on:	could move to:
b2	b3 or b4
e2	e3 or e4
h2	h3 or h4
The Black Pawn on:	could move to:
a7	a6 or a5
d7	d6 or d5
f7	f6 or f5

12. After a Pawn has moved the first time, it can go only one square ahead on each move after that. Answer Diagram 6 shows circles where the Pawns could move on their second moves. These squares are named, too.

A White Pawn on:	could move to:
b4	b5
e3	e4
h4	h5
A Black Pawn on:	could move to:
a6	a5
d5	d4
f5	f4

13. In Answer Diagram 7 a circle has been drawn around the other piece that the Pawn could capture, which is the Rook.

14. Yes, if Black advances the Pawn two squares, White can capture it *en passant* on the square d6.

15. No, Black will not lose the Pawn if it does not advance at all.

16. Yes, White can capture Black's Pawn if it advances one square. If Black's Pawn stays on d7, White's Pawn on c5 cannot capture it.

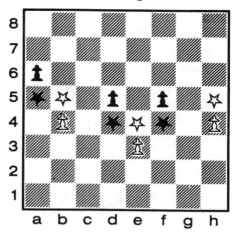

Answer Diagram 6

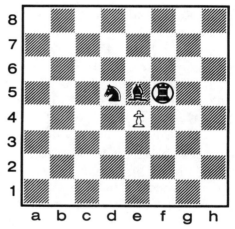

Answer Diagram 7

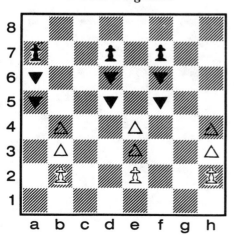

Answer Diagram 5

17. In Answer Diagram 12, two Black Pawns can be captured if they advance two squares. Black's b-Pawn can be taken by White's a-Pawn, and Black's f-Pawn can be taken by White's e-Pawn.

18. In Answer Diagram 16, Black's Knight on e6 could also take either White's d8-Queen, c7-Rook, c5-Bishop, or f4-Knight.

19. The Bishop could move along the c6–h1 diagonal.

20. The Bishop could take the Rook (Answer Diagram 20).

21. The Rook could move along the a-file, from a8 to a2, or it could move along the 8th rank, from a8 to h8.

22. The Rook could take either the a2-Pawn or the h8-Bishop (Answer Diagram 24).

23. The Queen could move to any of the following squares: d5, d6, d7, d8, d3, d2, d1, e4, f4, g4, h4, c4, b4, a4, c5, b6, a7, e3, f2, g1, e5, f6, g7, h8, c3, b2, a1 (Answer Diagram 26).

24. Black's Queen could capture any of the following pieces or Pawns: Queen at a2; Bishop at b6; Rook at c8; Knight at g8; Bishop at g6; Pawn at h3; Pawn at e2. See Answer Diagram 27.

25. On the next turn, the King could move to any of these squares: e5, f5, f4, f3, e3, d3, d4, and d5 (Answer Diagram 30).

26. The Black King could safely take only White's f5-Pawn. White's two Knights and the d4-Rook are protected and cannot be captured by Black's King (Answer Diagram 31).

27. White's King could safely move to any of these squares: d4, d3, e3, f3, and f4. See Answer Diagram 27, next page.

Black's King could safely move to d6, d7, e7, f7, and f6.

Neither King could move to d5, e5, or f5, because on those squares either King would be open to capture by the other.

Answer Diagram 12

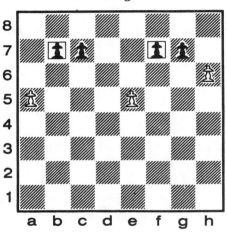

Answer Diagram 16

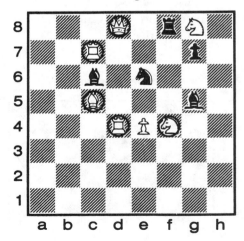

Answer Diagram 20

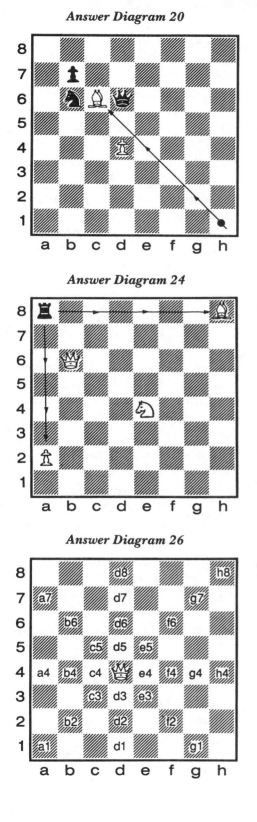

Answer Diagram 24

Answer Diagram 26

Answer Diagram 27

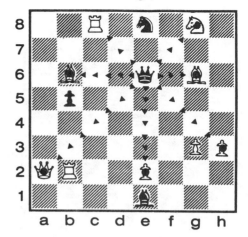

Answer Diagram 30

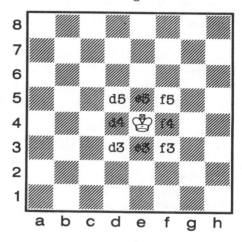

Answer Diagram 31

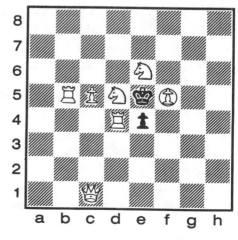

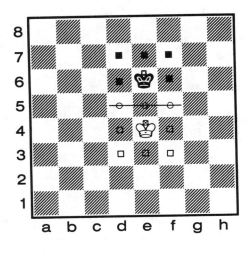

28. "Light on the right" means that at the start the board must have a light square in each player's right-hand corner. If you do not have a light square in the right-hand corner, then the Queens and Kings will be on the wrong squares.

29. There are 64 squares on the chessboard. There are 32 light squares and 32 dark ones.

30. At the start of a game, White's pieces line up on the chessboard from left to right in this way: Rook on a1; Knight on b1; Bishop on c1; Queen on d1; King on e1; Bishop on f1; Knight on g1; Rook on h1.

31. "Queen on her own color" means that at the start of a game, the Black Queen must be on a dark square (d8) and the White Queen must be on a light square (d1).

32. A Bishop is worth 3 points, which means it is also worth three Pawns.

33. A Knight is worth 3 points, which means it is also worth three Pawns.

34. A Queen is worth 9 points, which means it is also worth nine Pawns, which is equal to a Rook and four pawns, which is about equal to three minor pieces.

35. The Knight moves in the shape of the capital letter L. It is the only chessman that can jump over pieces and Pawns in regular play.

36. A Queen can move like a Bishop, a Rook, or a King. It can move forward or backward, to the left or to the right. It can move along diagonals in any direction. It cannot, however, jump over other pieces or Pawns, like a Knight.

37. Pawns can *never* move backward. Pawns can only move forward. The White Pawns move toward the Black Pawns and the Black Pawns move toward the White Pawns. That is why Pawns of both armies come closer and closer to each other as a game develops.

38. Rooks can move backward or forward, or to the right or left.

39. Every Pawn can move two squares on its first move only. After that, a Pawn can move forward only one square at a time.

40. Kings can move in any direction, backward or forward, up or down, but they can move only one square at a time. Kings can *never* move two squares, except when they *castle*. We will talk more about castling later.

41. There are two Kings on a chessboard, a Black King and a White King.

42. No, the Queen can *never* jump over other pieces or Pawns.

43. The Knight can jump over any other piece or Pawn, of either color.

44. No, you may never allow your King to be captured.

45. The King can *never* be captured, even if you move it to a bad square by mistake. If you make such a mistake, then that move has to be taken back and another move played.

46. White has eight pieces at the start of a chess game. They are two Rooks, two Knights, two Bishops, a Queen, and a King.

47. Black has 16 men at the start of a chess game. Besides the eight pieces, Black has eight Pawns, which also count as chessmen.

48. The Bishop and the Knight are the minor pieces.

49. The Rook and the Queen are the major pieces.

50. A rank is a line of squares going across the board. The squares along the ranks alternate between dark and light.

51. A file is a line of squares going up and down the board from bottom to top. The squares in a file alternate between dark and light.

52. A diagonal is a slanted line of squares connecting two sides or corners of the chessboard. Diagonals are made up of squares of only one color.

53. Most of the time, you would rather have a Rook than a Bishop. A Rook is worth five Pawns, and a Bishop is only worth three. A Rook is more valuable than a Bishop.

54. Most of the time, you would rather have a Queen than a Rook. A Queen is worth nine Pawns and a Rook is worth only five. A Queen is more valuable than a Rook.

55. Most of the time, you would rather have two Knights than one Rook. Two Knights are worth at least six pawns ($2 \times 3 = 6$). When they work together, they gain in value, so we can give the Knights a value of seven pawns. A Rook is worth only five Pawns. Two Knights working together are worth 2 points more than a Rook.

56. Most of the time, you would rather have a Queen than a Rook and Knight together, or a Rook and Bishop together. A Queen is worth nine Pawns, but a Rook and Knight together are worth only eight Pawns ($5 + 3 = 8$). A Rook and Bishop together are also worth only eight Pawns (or 8 points). A Queen by itself is worth more than a Rook and Knight together or a Rook and Bishop together.

57. To choose between having three minor pieces or a Queen alone, you would have to look very carefully at the position. Together, the three minor pieces (Knights and Bishops) are worth about nine Pawns, or the same as the Queen. In some cases you would rather have the Queen and in some the minor pieces.

58. Two Rooks are worth ten Pawns and the Queen is worth only nine. But in many cases, the two Rooks are about equal to a Queen.

59. Most of the time, you would rather have four Pawns than one Knight, which is worth only three Pawns.

60. Most of the time, you would rather have the Bishop, which is worth three Pawns.

Answers for Chapter 2

NOTE: Some answers have no diagram because the diagram that appears with the question is all you need.

1. Answer Diagram 36–1 shows the files as lines of squares going up and down the chessboard.

2. Answer Diagram 36–2 shows the ranks as lines of squares going across the chessboard.

3. The circled squares in Answer Diagram 37 are d4; f6; a1; b8; and h5.

4. In Answer Diagram 37, the names of these squares have been filled in: b1; e8; f4; and h2.

Answer Diagram 36–1

Black

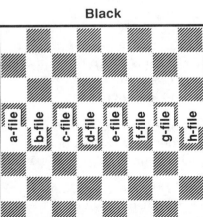

White

Answer Diagram 36–2

Black

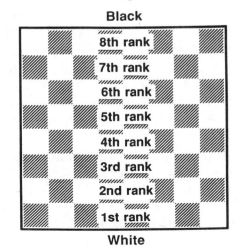

White

5. These squares have been crossed off in Answer Diagram 37: e4; h7; g2; and a7.

6. The White King is at g1.

7. The Black Queen is at e4.

8. The White Pawn is at f2.

9. The Black Pawn is at c6.

10. The White Bishop is at c1.

11. The Black Knight is at g8.

12. The White Rook is at b7.

13. The Black King is at e8.

14. White's eight Pawns are on a2, b2, c2, d2, e2, f2, g2, and h2.

15. Black's eight Pawns are on a7, b7, c7, d7, e7, f7, g7, and h7.

16. White's two Knights are on b1 and g1.

17. Black's two Knights are on b8 and g8.

18. White's two Bishops are on c1 and f1.

19. Black's two Bishops are on c8 and f8.

20. White's two Rooks are on a1 and h1.

21. Black's two Rooks are on a8 and h8.

22. White's Queen is on d1.

23. Black's Queen is on d8.

24. White's King is on e1.

25. Black's King is on e8.

26. You would say Nb1–c3 as "Knight on b1 to c3."

27. You would write "Queen on f5 to f8" as Qf5–f8.

28. You would say Kg8–f8 as "King on g8 to f8."

29. You would write "Rook on h6 to c6" as Rh6–c6.

30. You would say Nd6–e4 as "Knight on d6 to e4."

31. You would write "Bishop on f8 to g7" as Bf8–g7.

32. You would say e6–e5 as "Pawn on e6 to e5."

33. You would write "Pawn on a2 to a4" as a2–a4.

34. You would say h6–h7 as "Pawn on h6 to h7."

35. You would write "Pawn on d3 to d4" as d3–d4.

36. See Answer Diagram 41.

37. See Answer Diagram 41.

38. The King-Knight starts on g1 for White and g8 for Black. The King-Rook starts on h1 for White and h8 for Black.

Answer Diagram 37

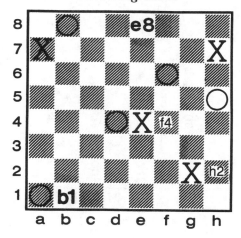

Answer Diagram 41

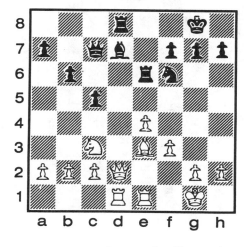

39. The Queen-Knight is on b1 for White and b8 for Black. The Queen-Rook is on a1 for White and a8 for Black.

40. The name of the piece that sits on f1 at the beginning of a game is the White King-Bishop.

41. The a-file is also the Queen-Rook file.

42. The b-file is also the Queen-Knight file.

43. The c-file is also the Queen-Bishop file.

44. The d-file is also the Queen-file.

45. The e-file is also the King-file.

46. The f-file is also the King-Bishop file.

47. The g-file is also the King-Knight file.

48. The h-file is also the King Rook file.

49. The Pawn on a2: algebraic name, a-Pawn; descriptive name, Queen-Rook Pawn.

50. The Pawn on c2: algebraic name, c-Pawn; descriptive name, Queen-Bishop Pawn.

51. The Pawn on d2: algebraic name, d-Pawn; descriptive name, Queen-Pawn.

52. The Pawn on e2: algebraic name, e-Pawn; descriptive name, King-Pawn.

53. The Pawn on f2: algebraic name, f-Pawn; descriptive name, King-Bishop Pawn.

54. The Pawn on g2: algebraic name, g-Pawn; descriptive name, King-Knight Pawn.

55. The Pawn on a7: algebraic name, a-Pawn; descriptive name, Queen-Rook Pawn.

56. The Pawn on b7: algebraic name, b-Pawn; descriptive name, Queen-Knight Pawn.

57. The Pawn on c7: algebraic name, c-Pawn; descriptive name, Queen-Bishop Pawn.

58. The Pawn on d7: algebraic name, d-Pawn; descriptive name, Queen-Pawn.

59. The Pawn on e7: algebraic name, e-Pawn; descriptive name, King-Pawn.

60. The Pawn on f7: algebraic name, f-Pawn; descriptive name, King-Bishop Pawn.

61. The Pawn on h7: algebraic name, h-Pawn; descriptive name, King-Rook Pawn.

62. The algebraic name of the file with the doubled Pawns is the g-file.

63. The descriptive name for this file is the King-Knight file.

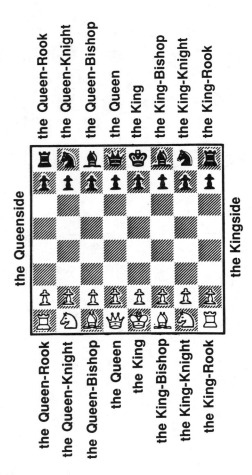

64. The algebraic name for the file that used to have the g5-Pawn on it is the h-file.

65. The descriptive name for this file is the King-Rook file.

66. Every square on the chessboard has a name. This way, we can know exactly which square we mean when we are discussing a chess position or when we are writing down a game.

67. Each square gets its name by combining the letter of its file with the number of its rank. For example, square a1 is the first square on the a-file.

68. At the start of a chess game the White Queen sits on d1.

69. At the start of a chess game the Black King sits on e8.

70. The rows of squares going across the chessboard from left to right are called ranks. The squares in a rank alternate between light and dark.

71. The ranks are the first rank, the second rank, the third rank, the fourth rank, the fifth rank, the sixth rank, the seventh rank, and the eighth rank.

72. The rows of squares going up and down the chessboard from bottom to top are called files. The squares in a file alternate between light and dark.

73. The files are the a-file, the b-file, the c-file, the d-file, the e-file, the f-file, the g-file, and the h-file.

74. In chess notation the N stands for Knight.

75. In chess notation the B stands for Bishop.

76. In chess notation the Q stands for Queen.

77. In chess notation you write R for Rook.

78. In chess notation you write K for King.

79. It is not always necessary to use a P to stand for Pawn in chess notation. So, to show a Pawn on square e4, we can just write e4.

80. In chess notation × stands for "takes," or "captures." If we write Bb1×Rf5, we mean the Bishop on the square b1 captures, or takes, the Rook on f5.

81. In chess notation + means "check," or "attacks the King."

82. White's moves are written in the left-hand column in chess notation. This is because we read from left to right and White always moves first.

83. In chess notation Black's moves are always written in the right-hand column.

84. You would write "Knight on b1 to c3" as Nb1–c3.

85. You would say c5×Rd4 as "Pawn on c5 takes Rook on d4."

86. The Kingside of Diagram 56, that is, the right half of the board, should be crossed out.

87. White's Queen-Rook should be circled in Diagram 56.

88. White's Queen-Rook sits on a1.

89. The Black Queen-Bishop should be on c8 in Diagram 56.

90. Black's Queen-Bishop is on c4.

91. White's Queen-Knight Pawn should be circled in Diagram 56.

92. White's QNP is on b2.

93. It is a b-Pawn.

94. Black's Queen-Rook Pawn should be circled in Diagram 56.

95. It is on a7.

96. It is an a-Pawn.

Answers for Chapter 3

1. White's King is on e4.

2. Black's Knight is on g6.

3. White's King does not threaten Black's Knight from the square e4, because it is two squares away from the Knight.

4. The King must go to the square f5 to threaten the Knight, as shown in Answer Diagram 57.

5. White's Bishop is on f1.

6. Black's Rook is on a8.

7. White's Bishop does not threaten Black's Rook from the square f1, because the Bishop is not yet on the a8–h1 diagonal.

8. The Bishop must go to the square g2 to threaten the Rook, as shown in Answer Diagram 58.

Answer Diagram 57

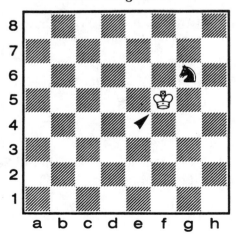

Answer Diagram 58

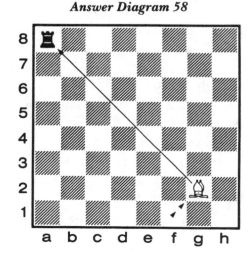

9. White's Rook is on e1.

10. Black's Pawn is on a3.

11. White's Rook does not threaten Black's Pawn from the square e1, because it is not yet on the a-file.

12. The Rook must go to the square a1 to threaten the Pawn, as shown in Answer Diagram 59. The Rook can't go to e3 to attack Black's Pawn because its own Pawn at e2 blocks the way.

13. White's Queen is on d1.

14. Black's Knight is on a8.

15. White's Queen does not threaten Black's Knight from the square d1, because d1 does not connect to a8 along any file, rank, or diagonal.

16. The Queen must go to the square d8 to threaten and *trap* the Knight and win it. The Queen could also *attack* the Knight by moving to a1, a4, d5, f3, or h1, but none of those moves *traps* the Knight. A piece is trapped when it is threatened and has no way to save itself.

    If you study Answer Diagram 60 you will see that the Knight has only two squares to which it can move, b6 and c7, and the Queen at d8 can take it on either of those squares, so the Knight is trapped.

17. White's Knight is on e5.

18. Black's Bishop is on b8.

19. White's Knight does not threaten Black's Bishop from the square e5 because it is too far away.

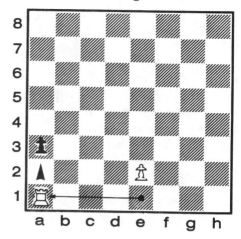

Answer Diagram 59

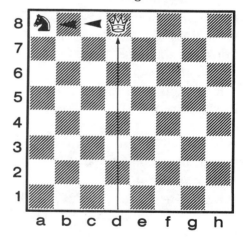

Answer Diagram 60

20. The Knight must go to the square c6 to threaten and trap the Bishop. The Knight could attack the Bishop from d7, too, but moving to d7 does not trap the Bishop. The Bishop could then escape to a7. If you study Answer Diagram 61 you will see that the Bishop has only one square to which it can move, a7, and the Knight at c6 can take it there too, so the Bishop is trapped.

21. White's Pawn is on g4.

22. Black's Rook is on h5.

23. Yes, White's Pawn does threaten Black's Rook from the square g4.

24. The Pawn does not have to go any-where to threaten the Rook. It already attacks the Rook from g4. If it is White's turn, White can actually cap-ture the Rook with the Pawn, as shown in Answer Diagram 62.

25. White's Bishop can threaten Black's Rook from a3 or e3, as shown in Answer Diagram 63.

26. White's Rook can threaten Black's Pawn from b1 or c7, as shown in Answer Diagram 64.

27. White's Knight can threaten Black's Queen from c6 or f7, as shown in Answer Diagram 65.

28. White's Queen can threaten Black's Knight from a8, b7, a1, g1, and h7, as shown in Answer Diagram 66.

29. Black can save the threatened Bishop on h7 by moving the Bishop to safety, either to f5, e4, d3, c2, or b1, as shown in Answer Diagram 67. But Black doesn't want to move the Bishop to g6 or g8, for White's Rook could then still take it.

30. The threatened man is a White Rook.

31. The threatened man sits on c3.

32. The threatened man is worth 5 points.

33. Black's Knight is the attacker.

34. The attacking Knight sits on d5.

35. The attacking Knight is worth 3 points.

36. Yes, the threatened man can be saved.

Answer Diagram 61

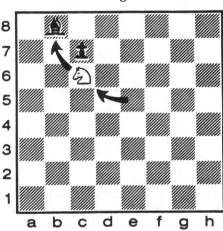

Answer Diagram 62

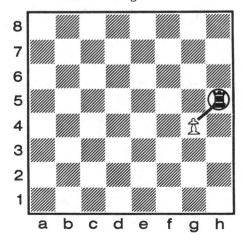

Answer Diagram 63

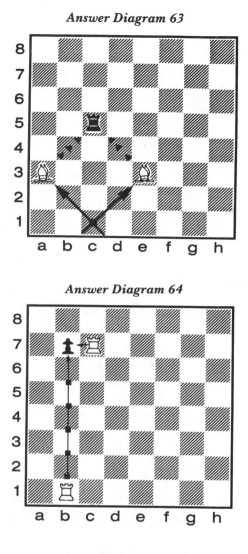

Answer Diagram 66

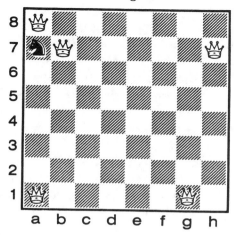

Answer Diagram 64

Answer Diagram 67

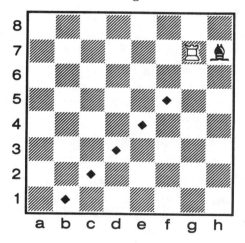

Answer Diagram 65

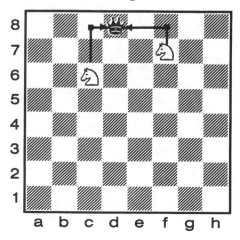

37. The threatened man (the Rook) can be saved by capturing the attacker (the Knight) with the g2-Bishop, as shown in Answer Diagram 68.

38. The threatened man should be saved, even though the Bishop that saves it can then be taken by the Black Pawn at e6. The threatened man is a Rook, worth 5 points, and the Bishop saving it is worth only 3 points. When the Bishop takes the Knight (also worth 3 points) White turns the threat of losing a Rook into an even trade of a Bishop for a Knight.

39. Yes, the Bishop can be moved to threaten the Knight, as shown by move 1 in Answer Diagram 69.

40. The White Bishop must move to g5 to threaten the Black Knight.

41. The Black Knight can be protected by moving the Rook from c8 to e8, as shown by move 2 in Answer Diagram 69.

42. The Bishop is worth 3 points.

43. The Knight is worth 3 points.

44. No, exchanging the Bishop for the Knight is an equal trade.

45. The White Bishop can *never* attack or threaten the Black Pawn as long as the Pawn stays on d6. A light-squared Bishop cannot directly attack a man on a dark square.

46. By moving the Bishop from d3 to e4, as shown in Answer Diagram 70. The Rook is then threatened along the a8–h1 diagonal.

47. The Rook is worth more than the Bishop, 5 points to 3.

48. The Rook can be saved by moving it away, off the a8–h1 diagonal.

49. Yes, the Black Pawn at e5 is under attack.

50. The Pawn is threatened by White's Rook.

51. Yes, the Pawn can be protected.

52. The e5-pawn can be protected with the f-pawn. The f-pawn should be moved from f7 to f6, as shown in Answer Diagram 71. If the Rook then took the e5-pawn, Black would take back with the f6-pawn and come out 4 points ahead, since a Rook is worth 5 points and a Pawn only 1.

53. There are two attackers, because the Black and White Pawns are attacking each other. If it is Black's move, Black can take the attacking White Pawn with the move g5×f4, as shown in Answer Diagram 72. Black could also save his pawn by moving it to g4.

54. There are two attackers, because the Black Bishop and White Queen are attacking each other. If it is Black's move, Black can take the attacking White Queen with the move Bb3×d1, as shown in Answer Diagram 73.

Answer Diagram 68

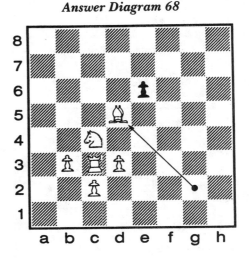

Answer Diagram 69

Answer Diagram 70

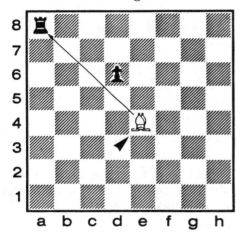

Answer Diagram 71

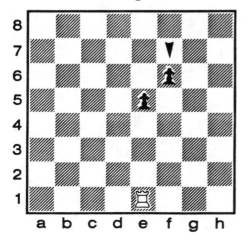

Answer Diagram 72

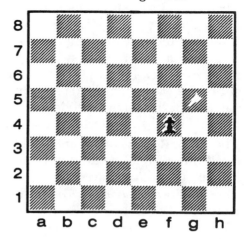

Answer Diagram 73

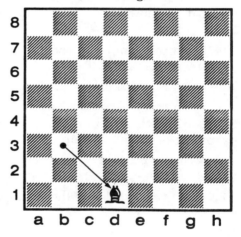

55. The Black Bishop is being attacked by the White Knight. If it is Black's move, Black can move away along the a6–f1 diagonal, as shown in Answer Diagram 74. Black's Bishop can also move out of the way along the d1–h5 diagonal, except that if the Bishop moves to square f3, the Knight can still take it.

56. The Black Rook is being attacked by the White King. The Rook can move away in any of four directions. One route is shown in Answer Diagram 75. However, if the Rook moves to square d5, d4, e6, or f6, it can still be taken by the King.

57. Yes, there is. You can move your Pawn forward, as shown in Answer Diagram 76.

58. The Pawn that can block the attack on the Queen sits on c7.

59. The Pawn is worth one point.

60. The Pawn could save the Queen by going to c6, where it blocks the diagonal attack of the b5-Bishop.

61. Yes, the Bishop could take the c6-Pawn.

62. The Pawn is worth 1 and the Bishop is worth 3.

63. Yes, the Queen would then protect the c6-pawn.

64. No, White cannot safely take the c6-pawn (the blocker) with the b5-Bishop.

65. Because the Black Queen would take back the Bishop once the Bishop captured on c6. Black would then win a Bishop worth 3 points for a pawn worth 1 point. Black would come out 2 points ahead.

66. The Queen would safely capture on c6, for nothing would be attacking it or about to attack it.

67. Attacked man and its square: The Black Rook on g7.

68. Attacker and its square: The White Bishop on b2.

69. Chessman that can block the attack: The Black Knight on e8, by moving to the position shown in Answer Diagram 77.

70. Square where the defender must move: f6.

71. Attacked man and its square: The Black Bishop on e5.

72. Attacker and its square: The White Rook on e1.

73. Chessman that can block the attack: The Black Rook on h4, by moving to the position shown in Answer Diagram 78.

74. Square where the defender must move: e4.

75. Attacked man and its square: The White Knight on d4.

76. Attacker and its square: The Black Bishop on b6.

77. Chessman that can block the attack: The White pawn on c4, by moving to the position shown in Answer Diagram 79.

Answer Diagram 74

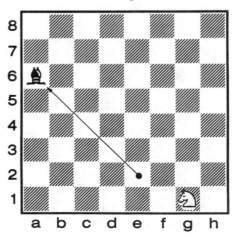

Answer Diagram 75

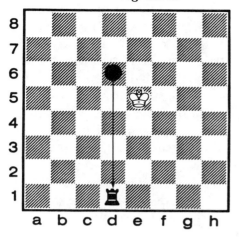

Answer Diagram 78

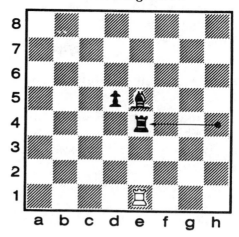

Answer Diagram 76

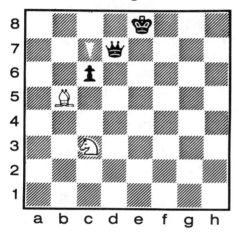

Answer Diagram 79

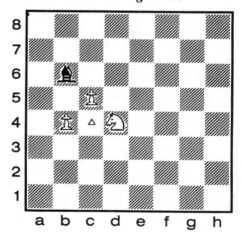

Answer Diagram 77

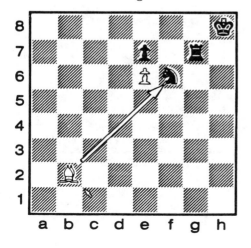

78. Square where the defender must move: c5.

79. Attacked man and its square: The White Queen on c3.

80. Attacker and its square: The Black Bishop on a5.

81. Chessman that can block the attack: The White pawn on b2, by moving to the position shown in Answer Diagram 80.

82. Square where the defender must move: b4.

83. Attacked man and its square: The White Rook on h1.

84. Attacker and its square: The Black Queen on d5.

85. Chessman that can block the attack: The White Knight on g1, by moving to the position shown in Answer Diagram 81.

86. Square where the defender must move: f3.

87. Attacked man and its square: The Black Bishop on d8.

88. Attacker and its square: The White Queen on a8.

89. Chessman that can block the attack: The Black Bishop on e6, by moving to the position shown in Answer Diagram 82.

90. Square where the defender must move: c8.

91. The Rook on a8 is attacked by a White Knight.

92. The attacking White Knight sits on c7.

93. The White Rook on c1 protects the c7-Knight.

94. The attacking Knight can be captured by the d6-Bishop, as shown in Answer Diagram 83–1.

95. The c7-Knight is worth 3 points.

96. Capturing the c7-Knight with the d6-Bishop does not win material. It only trades material, because the White Rook can then take the Black Bishop, as shown in Diagram 83–2.

97. It is only a trade because White can take back a piece of Black's, which is also worth 3 points. An even-Steven trade.

98. Yes, by trading Bishop for Knight, Black ends the attack to the a8-Rook, so the Rook is saved.

99. Attacked White man and square: The White Queen on d2.

100. Attacker and square: The Black Bishop on b4.

101. Can you capture the attacker and come out ahead? Yes. White's a3-Pawn can take the Bishop by moving to the position shown in Answer Diagram 84–1. Black can then take White's Pawn with either a Pawn or a Knight, but he still loses 2 points.

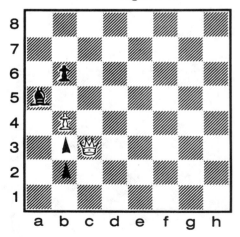

Answer Diagram 80

Answer Diagram 81

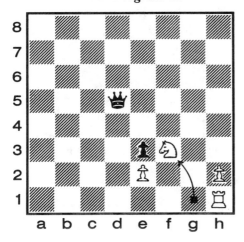

Answer Diagram 83–2

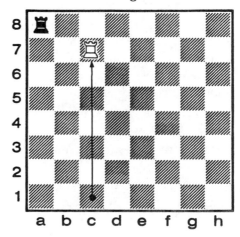

Answer Diagram 82

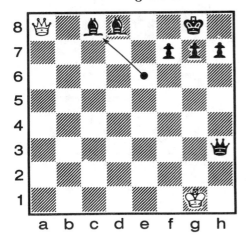

Answer Diagram 84–1

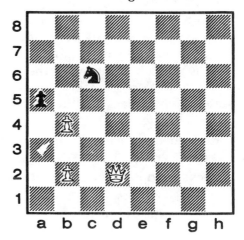

Answer Diagram 83–1

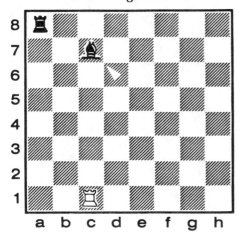

102. Will you win material? Yes. Even though Black can take back with a Pawn (as shown in Answer Diagram 84–2) or a Knight, White comes out 2 points ahead. Black gets a Pawn, but White gets a Bishop. White should make this trade.

103. Threatened man and its square: Black's Rook at h8.

104. Attacker and its square: White's Bishop on e5.

105. Can you capture the attacker and come out ahead? No. Black's Queen could take the White Bishop, as shown in Answer Diagram 85–1, but would be taken back by White's f3-Knight, as shown in Answer Diagram 85–2.

106. Will you win material? No. You will lose material, for the Bishop you take is worth 3 points while the Queen you lose is worth 9. Black will lose 6 points. Black should *not* make this exchange.

107. Threatened man and its square: The White Pawn on c3.

108. Attacker and its square: The Black Knight on e4.

109. Can you capture the attacker and come out ahead? Yes. The Pawn on d3 can make the capture, as shown in Answer Diagram 86–1. White comes out ahead after the Bishop takes back.

110. Will you win material? Yes. Even though Black can take back with the Bishop, as shown in Answer Diagram 86–2, winning White's pawn (worth 1 point), Black will have lost 3 points when the Knight was captured and will be behind 2 points on the exchange.

111. Threatened man and its square: Both the Black Knight on d7 and the Black Bishop on a6 are attacked, but only the Knight on d7 is threatened.

112. Attacker and its square: The White Bishop on b5.

113. Can you capture the attacker and come out ahead? No. Black can capture White's b5-Bishop with Black's a6-Bishop, as shown in Answer Diagram 87–1, but Black's Bishop is then under attack by White's Rook.

Answer Diagram 84–2

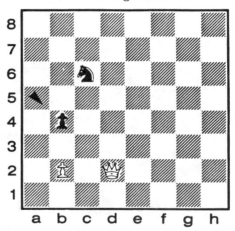

Answer Diagram 85–1

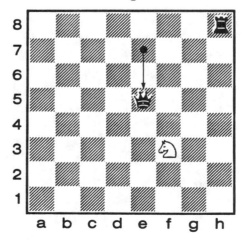

Answer Diagram 85–2

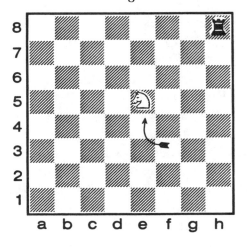

Answer Diagram 86–2

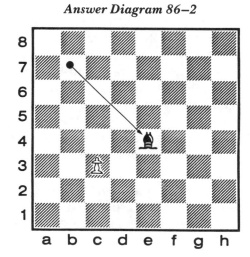

Answer Diagram 86–1

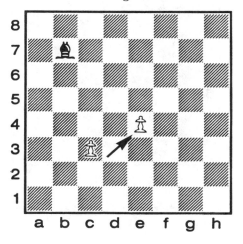

Answer Diagram 87–1

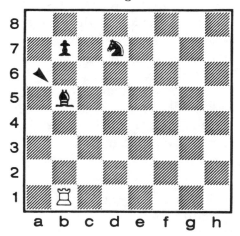

114. Will you win material? No. When White's b1–Rook takes Black's Bishop, as shown in Answer Diagram 87–2, each side has lost a Bishop, so it's an even trade of material. (In a game, a player who is already ahead in material will probably be glad to make such a trade, and a player who is behind in material will try to avoid one.)

115. Threatened man and its square: Again, two Black pieces attacked— the Queen on g3 and the Rook on f8.

116. Attacker and its square: The White Queen on a3.

117. Can you capture the attacker and come out ahead? No. Black's g3-Queen can take White's a3-Queen, as shown in Answer Diagram 88–1, but Black's Queen is then under attack by White's b2-Pawn.

118. Will you win material? No. When White's b2-pawn takes Black's Queen, as shown in Answer Diagram 88–2, it becomes an even trade, a Queen for a Queen, 9 points for 9 points, even-Steven.

119. Threatened man and its square: White's b2-Pawn.

120. Attacker and its square: Black's Bishop on g7.

121. Can you capture the attacker and come out ahead? No. White's g1-Rook can capture Black's g7-Bishop, as shown in Answer Diagram 89–1, but then White's Rook is under attack by Black's King.

122. Will you win material? No. You will lose material. After Black's f8-King has taken the Rook, as shown in Answer Diagram 89–2, White has gained the Bishop, worth 3 points,

but lost the Rook, worth 5 points. White comes out 2 points behind.

123. Yes. Black can defend the Knight with a Pawn.

124. The Pawn that can defend the Knight is on d7.

125. The Pawn should go to d6 (Answer Diagram 90).

126. Threatened man and its square: The Black Bishop on e7.

127. Attacker and its square: The White Rook on e1.

128. Piece that can defend the attacked chessman: The Black King.

Answer Diagram 87–2

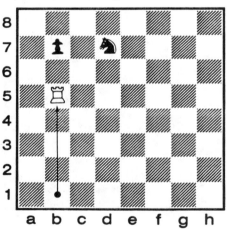

Answer Diagram 88–1

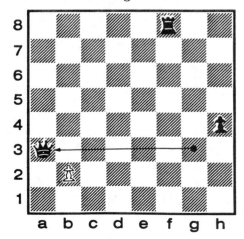

Answer Diagram 88–2

Answer Diagram 89–2

Answer Diagram 89–1

Answer Diagram 90

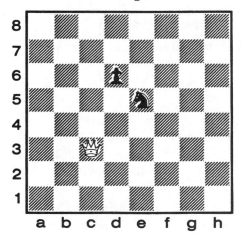

129. Square to which the defender must move: f8, as shown in Answer Diagram 91.

130. Threatened man and its square: The Black pawn on b5.

131. Attacker and its square: The White Rook on b1.

132. Piece that can defend the attacked chessman: The Black pawn on a7.

133. Square to which the defender must move: a6, as shown in Answer Diagram 92.

134. Threatened man and its square: The Black Pawn on e5.

135. Attacker and its square: The White Knight on f3.

136. Piece that can defend the attacked chessman: The Black Knight on b8.

137. Square to which the defender must move: c6, as shown in Answer Diagram 93–1, or d7, as shown in Answer Diagram 93–2.

138. Attacked man and its square: The White Pawn on g2.

139. Attacker and its square: The Black Rook on g8.

140. Man that can defend the attacked chessman: White's h2-Pawn—but not by moving itself. The attacked Pawn must move to where the h2-Pawn protects it.

141. Square to which the attacked man must move to be safe: g3, as shown in Answer Diagram 94. At g3, the g-Pawn is protected by the h2-Pawn.

142. Threatened man and its square: The White Knight at b1.

143. Attacker and its square: The Black Rook at a1.

144. Man that can defend the attacked chessman: The White Queen.

145. Square to which the defender must move: d1, as shown in Answer Diagram 95.

146. Threatened man and its square: White's pawn on h6.

147. Attacker and its square: The Black rook on h1.

148. Man that can defend the attacked chessman: The White b2-Bishop.

149. Square to which the defender must move: g7, as shown in Answer Diagram 96. The Bishop could also defend the Pawn from c1, but the Rook could take the Bishop at c1.

Answer Diagram 91

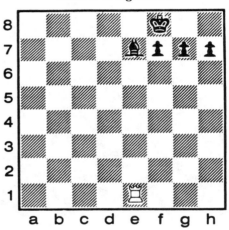

Answer Diagram 92

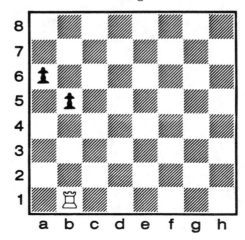

Answer Diagram 93–1

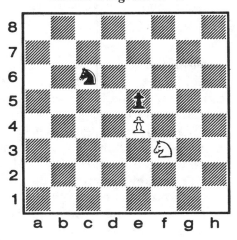

Answer Diagram 95

Answer Diagram 93–2

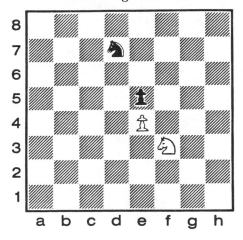

Answer Diagram 96

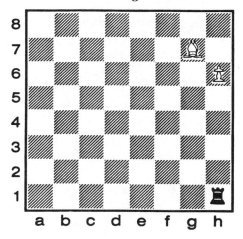

Answer Diagram 94

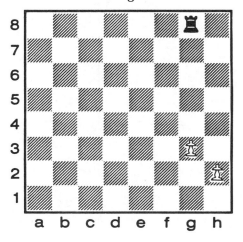

150. An attack is a threat to capture a piece or Pawn on the next move.

151. A trade is an exchange of chessmen of equal value.

152. Yes, you can save an attacked man by moving it, if there is a safe square.

153. Yes, you can save an attacked man by blocking the attack, especially if a man of lesser value can be put in the way.

154. Yes, you can save an attacked man by capturing the attacker.

155. Yes, you can save an attacked man by defending it, but not if the attacker is of less value than the attacked man. In that case, the attacker will capture the attacked man, whether it's guarded or not, because the attacker will come out ahead on the exchange.

156. No, you don't lose material in a trade, for your opponent loses some too. A trade usually means an exchange of losses of equal value. If you make an exchange and lose more material than your opponent does, you would not call it a trade but a mistake! Sometimes you are forced to make a bad exchange to avoid even worse trouble, and this is usually a forced exchange rather than a trade.

157. Yes, you can win material by capturing an attacker.

Answers for Chapter 4

1. Black is attacked by the White Rook at e1.

2. The Black piece under attack is the King.

3. Black can escape the attack from the Rook by moving to d8, as shown in Answer Diagram 97.

4. Yes, the White King is in check.

5. The Black Bishop at b4 is giving check.

6. White can escape the check by moving the White Knight from f3 to d2, as shown in Answer Diagram 98.

7. Yes, the White King at g1 is in check.

8. The Black Queen at d4 is giving check.

Answer Diagram 97

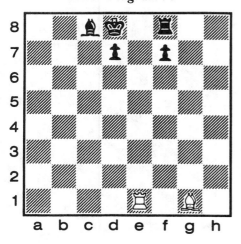

Answer Diagram 98

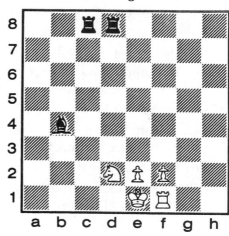

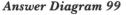

9. White can escape the check by moving the White King from g1 to h1, as shown in Answer Diagram 99.

10. Yes, the White King at c1 is in check.

11. The Black Knight at e2 is giving check.

12. White can escape the check by moving the White King from c1 to b1, as shown in Answer Diagram 100.

13. No, the White King is not in check.

14. No Black chessman is giving check.

15. No Black chessman is attacking the White King. However, White must move the King, because there is no other White piece to move, and there is only one place it can be moved—to a1, taking the Black Rook, as shown in Answer Diagram 101. Every other move would put the King in check and be illegal.

16. Yes, the White King at e1 is in check.

17. The Black Pawn at f2 is giving check.

18. White can escape the check by moving the White King from e1 to f1, as shown in Answer Diagram 102.

19. Yes, the White King at h1 is in check.

20. The Black Rook at e1 is giving check.

21. White can escape the check by moving the White King from h1 to h2, as shown in Answer Diagram 103.

22. White's Bishop on d5 is the attacker.

23. The Black King's safe square is h8, as shown in Answer Diagram 104.

24. White's Knight on b6 is the attacker.

25. The Black King's safe square is b8, as shown in Answer Diagram 105.

26. White's Rook on g1 is the attacker.

27. The Black King's safe square is h8, as shown in Answer Diagram 106.

28. White's Queen on h5 is the attacker.

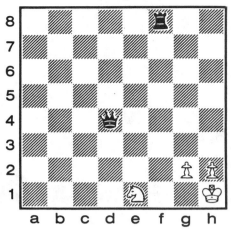

Answer Diagram 99

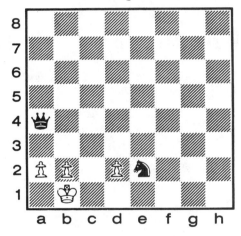

Answer Diagram 100

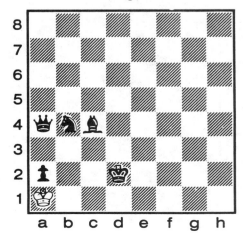

Answer Diagram 101

Answer Diagram 102

Answer Diagram 105

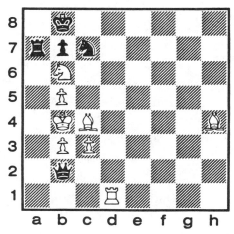

Answer Diagram 103

Answer Diagram 106

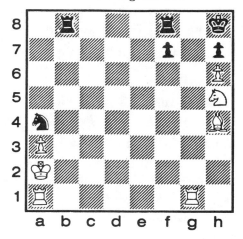

Answer Diagram 104

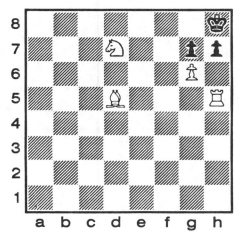

29. The Black King's safe square is f8, as shown in Answer Diagram 107.

30. White's King on e1 is in check.

31. Black's Rook on e8 is giving check.

32. Yes, the check can be blocked.

33. White's Bishop can block the check by moving from f1 to e2, as shown in Answer Diagram 108.

34. White's King on b1 is in check.

35. Black's Rook on d1 is giving check.

36. Yes, the check can be blocked.

37. White's Rook on c5 can block the check by moving from c5 to c1, as shown in Answer Diagram 109.

38. Black's King on a5 is in check.

39. White's Queen on a3 is giving check.

40. Yes, the check can be blocked.

41. Black's Queen can block the check by moving from e8 to a4, as shown in Answer Diagram 110.

42. White's King on h1 is in check.

43. Black's Bishop on b7 is giving check.

44. Yes, the check be blocked.

45. White's Knight can block the check by moving from g1 to f3, as shown in Answer Diagram 111.

46. Black's King on h7 is in check.

47. White's Pawn on g6 is giving check.

48. No, the attack cannot be blocked. A Pawn check can never be blocked. The only ways to get out of check from a Pawn are to capture the Pawn or move the King.

49. No piece can block the check. However, the King can get out of check by capturing the Pawn at g6, as shown in Answer Diagram 112.

50. Black's Knight at g3 is giving check.

51. White's Pawn can capture the enemy by moving from h2 to g3, as shown in Answer Diagram 113.

52. The enemy Knight is worth 3 points, and the Pawn that can capture it is worth 1 point.

53. No, the enemy cannot take the Pawn back.

54. You will gain 3 points.

55. Black's Bishop at c3 is giving check.

Answer Diagram 107

Answer Diagram 108

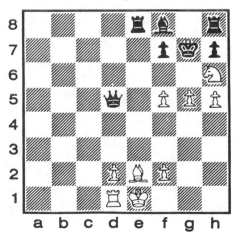

Answer Diagram 109

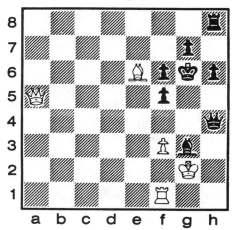

Answer Diagram 112

Answer Diagram 110

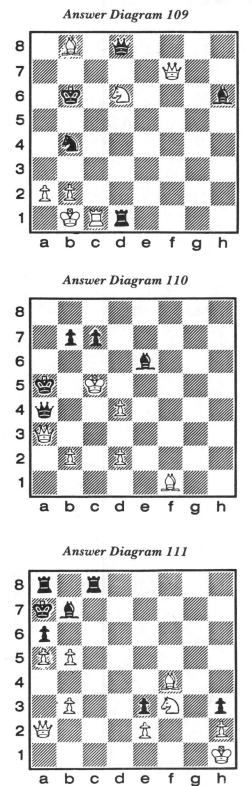

Answer Diagram 113

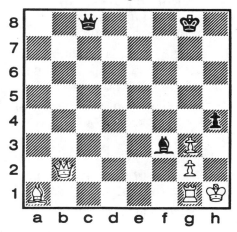

Answer Diagram 111

56. White's b-Knight can capture the enemy Bishop by moving from b5 to c3, as shown in Answer Diagram 114–1.

57. The enemy Bishop is worth 3 points, and the White Knight that can capture it is worth 3 points.

58. Yes, the enemy can take back with the Black Queen, as shown in Answer Diagram 114–2.

59. It's an even trade. The 3 points each side takes equals the 3 points each side loses.

60. Black's Rook at f8 is giving check.

61. White's Bishop can capture the enemy Rook by moving from c5 to f8, as shown in Answer Diagram 115–1.

62. The enemy Rook is worth 5 points, and the White Bishop that can capture it is worth 3 points.

63. Yes, the enemy can take back with the Black a8-Rook, as shown in Answer Diagram 115–2.

64. White takes a Rook worth 5 points and loses a Bishop worth 3 points, so you gain 2 points.

65. Black's Pawn at f2 is giving check.

66. White's King can capture the checking Pawn by moving from e1 to f2, as shown in Answer Diagram 116.

67. The enemy Pawn is worth 1 point, but the King capturing the enemy is worth *everything*. If you lose the King you lose the game.

68. No. If the enemy could take back, White's capture with the King would be against the rules. You are not allowed to move your King to a square where it can be captured.

69. White gains 1 point and loses none.

70. Black's Bishop at f3 is giving check.

71. White's g-Knight can capture the checking Bishop by moving from g5 to f3, as shown in Answer Diagram 117.

72. The enemy Bishop is worth 3 points, and the White Knight that can capture it is worth 3 points.

73. Yes, the enemy can take back with the Black Rook on f8. But probably Black wouldn't do it!

74. If Black's Rook takes White's Knight each side will have taken a piece worth 3 points, an even trade. But White's King can then take Black's Rook, which is worth 5 points. Black cannot take back, so White comes out ahead by 5 points. See if you can imagine all this happening as you look at Answer Diagram 117: Black's move is Rf8 × f3, and White's reply is Kg2 × f3. If Black's Rook *doesn't* take White's Knight, then White gains Black's Bishop for nothing, and comes out ahead by 3 points.

75. Black's Knight on f3 is giving check.

Answer Diagram 114–1

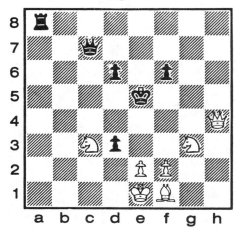

Answer Diagram 114–2

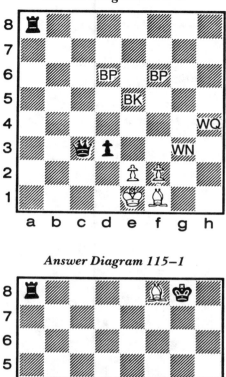

Answer Diagram 116

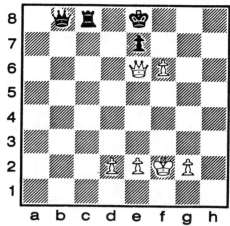

Answer Diagram 115–1

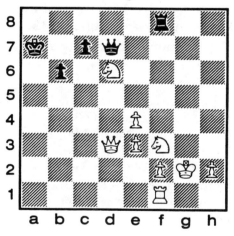

Answer Diagram 117

Answer Diagram 115–2

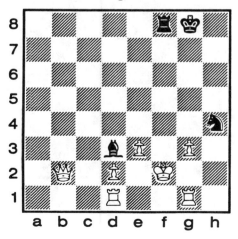

76. White's g-Pawn can capture the enemy Knight by moving from g2 to f3, as shown in Answer Diagram 118.

77. The enemy Knight is worth 3 points, and the White Pawn that can capture it is worth 1 point.

78. Yes, the enemy can take back with the Queen. By this time you should be able to see this without a diagram showing the move.

79. White will wind up 2 points ahead, winning a Knight but losing a Pawn.

80. Yes, you can check the Black King.

81. You can give check with the Rook that is on d1.

82. By moving the Rook from d1 to g1, as shown in Answer Diagram 119.

83. Yes, you can check the Black King.

84. You can give check with the Bishop that is on d5.

85. White gives check with the Bishop— but not by moving the Bishop! Rather by moving the Pawn out of the Bishop's way. This is called a *discovered check*. When White moves the Pawn from e6 to e7, White's Bishop gives a discovered check, as shown in Answer Diagram 120.

86. Yes, you can check the Black King.

87. You can give check with the Queen that is on d1.

88. By moving the Queen from d1 to h5, as shown in Answer Diagram 121. (Do you want to do it? Think about it carefully!)

89. Yes, you can check the Black King.

90. You can give check with the Knight that is on f5.

91. By moving the Knight from f5 to d6, as shown in Answer Diagram 122.

92. No, you cannot check the Black King.

93. No man is able to move into position to give check to Black's King.

94. No check can be given next move.

95. Yes, White's Pawn on g6 can give check on the next move.

96. The Pawn must move to g7 to give check, as shown in Answer Diagram 124.

97. Yes, White's Rook on f1 can give check on the next move.

Answer Diagram 118

Answer Diagram 119

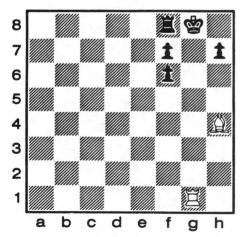

Answer Diagram 120

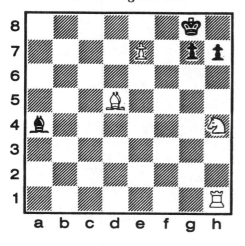

Answer Diagram 122

Answer Diagram 121

Answer Diagram 124

98. The Rook must move to e1 to give check, as shown in Answer Diagram 125.

99. Yes, White's Knight can give check on the next move.

100. The Knight must move to g6 to give check, as shown in Answer Diagram 126.

101. No, White's Bishop cannot check on the next move.

102. There is no way the Bishop can check as long as the Black King stays on a light square, because the Bishop travels only on dark squares. However, by moving to h6, as shown in Answer Diagram 127, the Bishop can create a very dangerous situation for Black. Do you see it?

103. Yes, White's Queen on e2 can give check on the next move.

104. White's Queen can give check by moving to a2, c4, e6, g2, or g4. You should be able to imagine these positions without the help of an Answer Diagram.

105. White's Rook on b8 is giving check to Black's King.

106. Black can save the King by blocking on f8 with the Bishop, as shown in Answer Diagram 129.

107. White's Bishop is giving check to Black's King.

108. Black can save the King by capturing White's Bishop with the Pawn, as shown in Answer Diagram 130.

109. White's Queen on a6 is giving check to Black's King.

110. Black can get out of check by moving the King to b8, as shown in Answer Diagram 131.

111. White's Pawn on f7 is giving check to Black's King.

112. Black can save the King by capturing White's Pawn with the Rook, as shown in Answer Diagram 132.

113. White's Bishop on b5 is giving check to Black's King.

114. Black cannot save the King. It is checkmate!

115. An attack on the King is against the rules: False.

116. An attack on the King is a check: True.

Answer Diagram 125

Answer Diagram 126

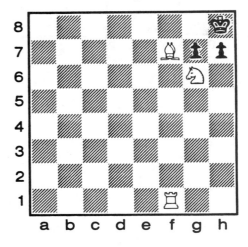

Answer Diagram 127

Answer Diagram 131

Answer Diagram 129

Answer Diagram 132

Answer Diagram 130

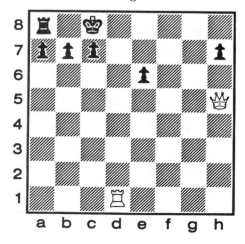

117. You can play any move you want when your King is in check: False.

118. You must get your King out of check before you play any other move: True.

119. You can get your King out of check only by capturing the attacker: False. There may be other ways.

120. You can get your King out of check only by moving it to a safe square: False. You might be able to save your King by moving it to a safe square, by capturing the attacker, or by blocking the attack.

121. Only the White King can check the Black King: False. Any White piece or Pawn is permitted to check the Black King, *except* the White King. It can never get close enough to the Black King to give check, since the two Kings must always stay a square apart.

122. Only a Queen can save a King: False. Any piece or Pawn may save the King if able.

123. When the King is in check the game is over: False. The King can usually get out of check.

124. You can only check a King on a dark square. False. If you are able, you can check a King on any square on the chessboard.

125. A CHECK is an attack on the King.

126. You can get your King out of check in THREE different ways.

127. You can get your King out of check by MOVING it to a safe square.

128. You can get your King out of check by moving another man between the KING and the attacker.

129. You can get your King out of check by CAPTURING the attacker.

130. If you cannot get your King out of CHECK the game is over.

131. If your King is in check you CAN-NOT make any other move before you save it.

132. If your King is in check you must get it OUT of check or you have lost the game.

133. You may get your King out of CHECK by blocking the attack.

134. You may GET your King out of check by capturing the attacker.

Answers for Chapter 5

1. Yes, White's King is in check.

2. Black's Bishop on b4 is checking White's King.

3. No, White's King does not have a safe move.

4. No, none of White's men can block the check.

5. No, White cannot capture Black's checking Bishop.

6. Yes, White's King is checkmated.

7. Black's Rook on e8 is checking White's King.

8. The White King cannot escape to a safe square.

9. The check cannot be blocked.

10. The checking Rook cannot be captured.

11. It is checkmate.

12. Black's Knight on h3 is checking White's King.

13. The White King cannot escape to a safe square. The Bishop guards both g2 and h1, so the King can't go to either square.

14. The check cannot be blocked.

15. The checking Knight cannot be captured.

16. It is checkmate.

17. Black's Knight on f2 is checking White's King.

18. The White King cannot escape to a safe square.

19. The check cannot be blocked.

20. The checking Knight can be captured by White's Bishop, as shown in Answer Diagram 137.

21. It is not checkmate.

22. Black's Rook on a1 is checking White's King.

23. The White King cannot escape to a safe square.

24. The checking Rook cannot be blocked.

25. The checking Rook cannot be captured.

26. It is checkmate.

27. Black's Queen on g2 is checking White's King.

28. The White King cannot escape to a safe square.

29. The checking Queen cannot be blocked.

30. The checking Queen cannot be captured by White's King because it is protected by the Bishop.

31. It is checkmate.

32. Black's Pawn on h2 is checking White's King.

33. The White King cannot escape to a safe square.

34. The checking Pawn cannot be blocked.

35. The checking Pawn cannot be captured because it is protected by the Knight.

36. It is checkmate.

37. Nothing is checking White's King.

38. The White King has two available squares. It can move to either h1 or f1.

39. There is no check to block.

40. There is no checking attacker to capture.

41. It is not checkmate.

42. Two men are checking the White King: Black's Knight on g3 and Bishop on a8. This is called double check. The only way to get out of double check is to move the King.

43. The White King cannot escape to a safe square.

44. The checking attackers cannot both be blocked. If White blocks the Bishop, White will still be in check from the Knight. A Knight cannot be blocked anyway, because it leaps over other men. Even when neither of the attackers is a Knight, there is no way to block two attackers at once.

45. The checking attackers cannot both be captured. If White captures the Bishop, the Knight still checks. If White captures the Knight, the Bishop still checks. There is no way to capture two attackers at once.

46. It is checkmate.

47. Black's Queen on h8 is giving check.

48. The White King cannot escape to a safe square.

49. The checking Queen cannot be blocked.

50. The checking Queen cannot be captured.

51. It is checkmate.

52. The winning move is Rc1–c8, which is read "Rook on c1 to c8." It is mate, because Black's King would be captured on the next move by White's Rook (see Answer Diagram 144).

53. The winning move is Qd3–h7, which is read "Queen on d3 to h7." It is mate because Black's King would be captured on the next move by White's Queen (see Answer Diagram 145). The Queen is guarded by the Bishop.

54. The winning move is Nh6–f7, which is read "Knight on h6 to f7." It is mate because Black's King would be captured on the next move by White's Knight (see Answer Diagram 146). This is called a *smothered mate*, because the Knight "smothers" the King.

Answer Diagram 145

Answer Diagram 137

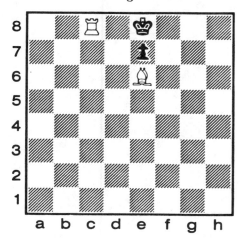

Answer Diagram 144

Answer Diagram 146

55. The winning move is Qa1–g7, which is read "Queen on a1 to g7." The Queen mates (see Answer Diagram 147).

56. The winning move is h6–h7, which is read "h6 to h7." The Pawn mates (see Answer Diagram 148).

57. The winning move is Bb1–a2, which is read "Bishop on b1 to a2." The Bishop mates (see Answer Diagram 149).

58. The winning move is Rg1–g8, which is read "Rook on g1 to g8." The Rook mates (see Answer Diagram 150).

59. The winning move is Qh1–a8, which is read "Queen on h1 to a8." The Queen mates (see Answer Diagram 151).

60. The winning move is Ra7–g7, which is read "Rook on a7 to g7." The a7-Rook mates (see Answer Diagram 152).

61. The winning move is Bg2×b7, which is read "Bishop on g2 takes on b7." The Bishop mates (see Answer Diagram 153).

62. Move the Black Bishop to h3, as shown in Answer Diagram 155.

Answer Diagram 148

Answer Diagram 149

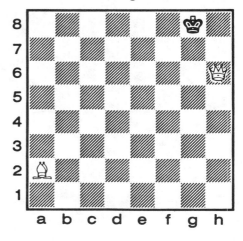

Answer Diagram 147

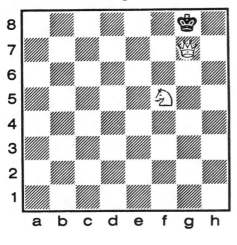

Answer Diagram 150

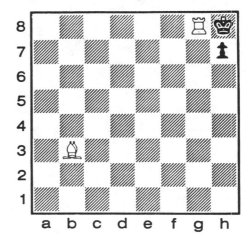

Answer Diagram 151

Answer Diagram 153

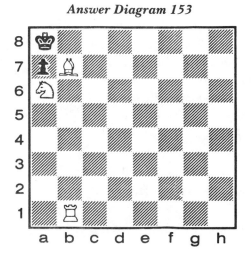

Answer Diagram 152

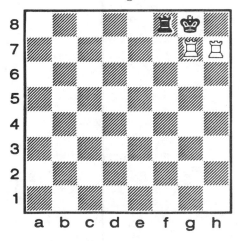

Answer Diagram 155

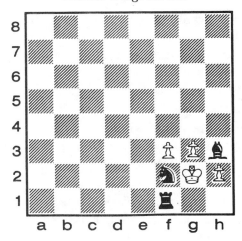

63. Move the Black Knight to g4, as shown in Answer Diagram 156.

64. Move the Black Rook to e1, as shown in Answer Diagram 157.

65. Move the Black Queen to h2, as shown in Answer Diagram 158.

66. Move the Black Pawn to f2, as shown in Answer Diagram 159.

67. No, the White King is not under attack.

68. No, the White King does not have a safe move.

69. White does not have a legal move. It is stalemate.

70. Yes, the White King is under attack.

71. No, the White King does not have a safe move.

72. White has no legal move. It is checkmate.

73. No, the White King is not under attack.

74. No, the White King does not have a safe move.

75. White has no legal move. It is stalemate.

76. No, the White King is not under attack.

77. No, the White King does not have a safe move.

78. White has a legal move. The Bishop at a7 can move to b8. It is Black who is checkmated.

79. Yes, the White King is under attack.

80. No, the White King does not have a safe move.

81. No, White doesn't have a legal move. It is checkmate.

82. No, Black doesn't have any legal moves.

83. It is checkmate.

84. No, Black doesn't have any legal moves.

85. It is stalemate.

86. No, Black doesn't have any legal moves.

87. It is checkmate.

88. Yes, Black has a legal move.

89. It is check. Black can get out of check, as shown in Answer Diagram 169.

90. Yes, Black has legal moves. One of them is shown in Answer Diagram 170. Can you find another?

91. It is just Black's move. Black is not in check, checkmate, or stalemate.

92. No, Black doesn't have any legal moves.

93. It is stalemate.

94. No, Black doesn't have any legal moves.

95. It is stalemate.

96. No, Black doesn't have any legal moves.

97. It is checkmate.

98. Yes, Black has a legal move.

Answer Diagram 156

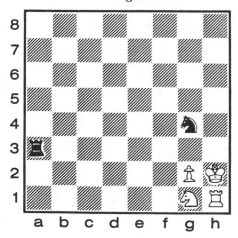

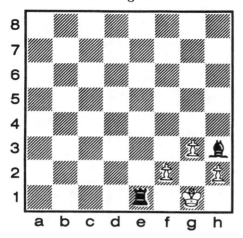

Answer Diagram 157

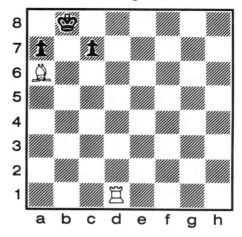

Answer Diagram 169

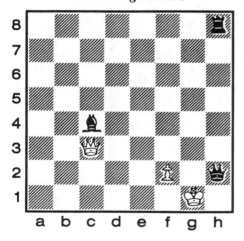

Answer Diagram 158

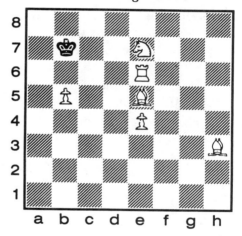

Answer Diagram 170

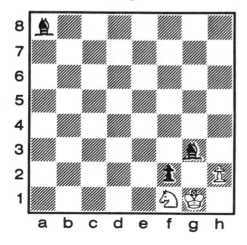

Answer Diagram 159

99. It is check. Black can move out of check as shown in Answer Diagram 174.

100. No, Black doesn't have a legal move.

101. It is checkmate.

102. CHECKMATE is an attack on the King which cannot be stopped.

103. The game of chess is won by mating the enemy KING.

104. It is MATE when the King in check has no safe square.

105. Mate is an attack which cannot be STOPPED.

106. Checkmate means THE GAME IS OVER.

107. If the King is not in check and neither the King nor any of its comrades have a legal move, it is STALEMATE.

108. In stalemate, no one WINS and no one LOSES.

109. Stalemate is also called a DRAW.

110. A draw is a TIE.

111. If the King is CHECKMATED it is under attack; if it is STALEMATED it is not under attack.

112. If you checkmate the enemy King you WIN the game.

113. If you stalemate the enemy King you do not WIN the game.

Answer Diagram 174

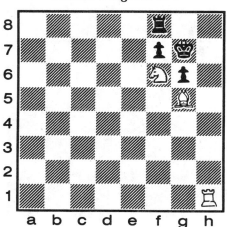

Answers for Chapter 6

1. Yes, White's new Queen would have all the powers of a natural Queen. It would move and capture the same way.

2. White's new Queen could check, attack, and defend just as a regular Queen can.

3. Yes, White's new Queen could give mate as would an ordinary Queen.

4. The Pawn sits on c7.

5. The Pawn may become either a Queen, Rook, Bishop, or Knight. It cannot become a King. No one is allowed to have two Kings.

6. Yes, you may have two Queens on the board at the same time. You may have as many as nine Queens—the original one and eight new ones.

7. There is no way for Black to get out of check after the Pawn promotes to a Queen. Black is checkmated, as shown in Answer Diagram 179–1.

Answer Diagram 179–1

8. The Pawn could also mate by becoming a Rook, as shown in Answer Diagram 179–2.

9. The promotion square is d8.

10. White should promote to a Queen, as shown in Answer Diagram 180.

11. Black's Queen must take White's Queen to stop mate.

12. A Rook would be as good as a Queen in this position.

13. The promotion square is a8.

14. White should promote to a Queen, as shown in Answer Diagram 181–1.

15. Black has to block the check by moving his Bishop to f8, as shown in Answer Diagram 181–2.

16. The promotion square is f8.

17. White should make a Knight! That checkmates Black, as shown in Answer Diagram 182–1. If White instead makes a Queen, as in Answer Diagram 182–2, then Black turns the tables and checkmates White. Promoting to a piece less valuable than a Queen is called *underpromotion.*

18. The promotion square is c8.

19. White should make a Rook, as shown in Answer Diagram 183. After Black then moves his King to a6, White's Rook moves to a8, giving mate.

20. Making a Queen stalemates Black. The game would then be drawn.

21. There are two promotion squares: b8 and c8. White can move (in chess, we call this forward movement of a Pawn an advance) his Pawn to c8 or capture with it on b8.

Answer Diagram 180

Answer Diagram 181–1

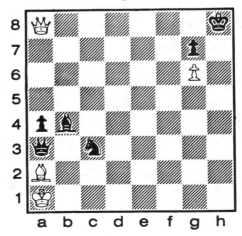

Answer Diagram 181–2

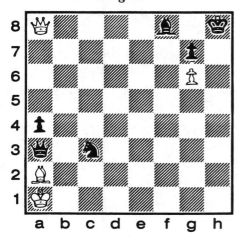

Answer Diagram 182–2

Answer Diagram 182–1

Answer Diagram 183

22. If White advances the Pawn to c8, it should be made into a Knight by underpromotion. Making a Knight on c8 checkmates Black's King, as shown in Answer Diagram 184–1. If White captures on b8, the Pawn should be made into a new Queen by promotion (as in Answer Diagram 184–2) or a new Bishop by underpromotion (as in Answer Diagram 184–3). In either case Black's King at a7 is checkmated. So, in this position, White with one move can mate in three different ways.

23. It doesn't matter which promotion you choose. All three mate in one move, so all three are equally good.

24. Yes, the Pawn should become a Queen.

25. If the Pawn becomes a Queen, White is mated, as shown in Answer Diagram 188.

26. The Pawn should not become a Knight.

27. If the Pawn becomes a Knight, it is not mate. White can then checkmate Black by moving the White Queen to d8.

28. The Pawn should become a Queen.

29. If the Pawn becomes a Queen, it is not mate. It is check, and Black's new Queen also attacks White's Rook on a5. This is a double attack. It is called a *fork*.

30. The Pawn should not become a Knight.

31. If the Pawn becomes a Knight, it is not mate. It is White's turn and material is even, White has a Rook and a Bishop and Black has a Knight, a Bishop, and two Pawns.

32. No, the Pawn should not become a Queen.

33. If the Pawn becomes a Queen, White is not mated. Instead, White can checkmate Black, by moving the Rook at c7 to c8.

34. The Pawn should become a Knight.

35. If the Pawn becomes a Knight it is mate to the White King, as shown in Answer Diagram 190.

36. No, the Pawn should not become a Queen.

37. If the Pawn becomes a Queen, White moves and mates Black.

38. The Pawn should become a Knight.

Answer Diagram 184–1

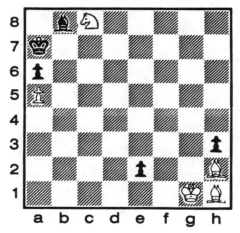

Answer Diagram 184–2

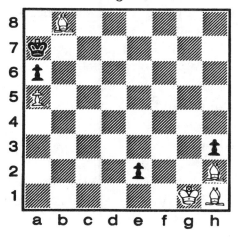

Answer Diagram 188

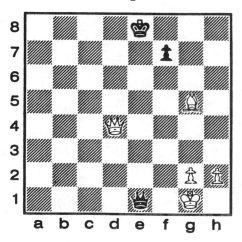

Answer Diagram 184–3

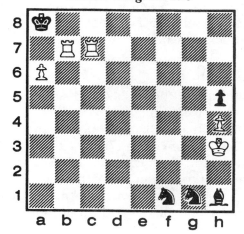

Answer Diagram 190

39. If the Pawn becomes a Knight it is not mate. But it is check to the White King. The new Knight also attacks White's Queen, as shown in Answer Diagram 191. That's a fork. After White gets the King out of check, Black's Knight captures White's Queen. Black is then ahead in material by 3 points. If Black makes a new Queen instead of a new Knight, both sides will have a Queen. By making less, Black winds up with more and avoids getting mated.

40. No, the Black Pawn should not become a Queen.

41. If the Black Pawn becomes a Queen, it is not mate. Instead, White checkmates Black. White would play Knight on e5 to f7. Then Black's King has no escape and Black cannot take the attacking Knight.

42. No, the Pawn should not become a Knight.

43. If the Black Pawn becomes a Knight, White is not in checkmate. Instead, White mates Black by moving the Knight from e5 to f7. The correct move for Black is not to promote at all, but to take on h2 with his Queen, giving mate, as shown in Answer Diagram 192. Black's Bishop supports the checkmating Queen.

44. The White King is on the square e1, the King's original square.

45. White has Pawns on the d-file and f-file, but no Pawns in front of the White King on the open e-file to block checks to White's King.

46. Yes. Black wants to check White's King along the open e-file with his Rook on f8. (A file is open if it has no Pawns on it.)

47. White's Rooks are on the squares a1 and h1.

48. The Black King is on the square g8. It is not the Black King's original square.

49. There are three Pawns in front of the Black King, one on f7, one on g7, and one on h7. These Pawns shelter Black's King and stop enemy checks.

50. No White chessman is able to check Black on the next move.

51. Black's Rooks are on a8 and f8.

52. White is not in check.

53. White would not have to castle through check.

54. White would not be castling into check.

55. There are no pieces in the way.

56. The King and Rook are on their original squares.

57. White can castle Kingside, as shown in Answer Diagram 204.

58. White is not in check.

59. White would not have to castle through check.

60. White would not be castling into check.

61. There are no pieces in the way.

62. The King and Rook are on their original squares.

63. White can castle Queenside, as shown in Answer Diagram 205.

64. White is not in check.

65. White would not have to castle through check.

66. White would not be castling into check.

67. There are no pieces in the way.

68. The King and Rooks are on their original squares.

Answer Diagram 191

Answer Diagram 204

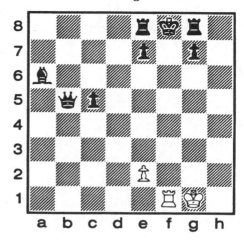

Answer Diagram 192

Answer Diagram 205

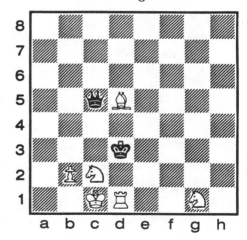

69. White can castle either Kingside, as shown in Answer Diagram 206–1, or Queenside, as shown in Answer Diagram 206–2.

70. White is in check from Black's Bishop at b4.

71. White would not have to castle through check.

72. White would not be castling into check.

73. There are no pieces in the way.

74. The King and Rook are on their original squares.

75. White cannot castle. You can't castle if in check. White should block the Bishop's check by c2 to c3, as shown in Answer Diagram 207. White then might be able to castle later.

76. White is not in check.

77. White would have to castle through check. Black's Bishop guards f1, a square the King would have to pass over.

78. White would not be castling into check.

79. There are no pieces in the way.

80. The King and Rook are on their original squares.

81. White cannot castle until the diagonal of the Black Bishop on a6 is blocked so that the Bishop no longer guards f1.

82. White is not in check.

83. White would not have to castle through check.

84. White would not be castling into check.

85. There are no pieces in the way.

86. The King is on its original square. The Rook is not.

87. White cannot castle. You are not permitted to castle with a Rook that has already moved.

88. White is not in check.

89. White would not have to castle through check.

90. White would be castling into check. Black's Rook guards g1, the square White's King would land on after castling Kingside.

91. There are no pieces in the way.

92. The King and Rook are on their original squares.

93. White cannot castle Kingside until Black's Rook moves off the g-file, is blocked, or is captured.

94. White is not in check.

95. White would not have to castle through check on the Queenside.

96. No, but White would be castling through check if he castled Kingside. Black's Knight guards f1.

97. There are no pieces in the way.

98. The King and both Rooks are on their original squares.

99. White can castle Queenside, as shown in Answer Diagram 211. White cannot castle Kingside.

100. White is not in check.

101. White would not have to castle through check. Black's Rook guards b1, but White's King never passes over that square.

102. White would not be castling into check.

103. There are no pieces in the way of Queenside castling. There is a Bishop sitting on f1, preventing Kingside castling.

104. The King and both Rooks are on their original squares.

Answer Diagram 206–1

Answer Diagram 207

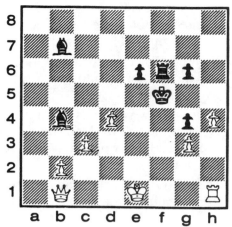

Answer Diagram 206–2

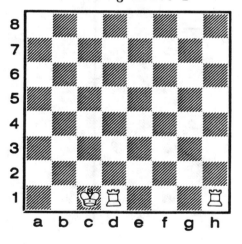

Answer Diagram 211

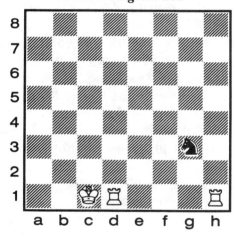

105. White can castle Queenside, as shown in Answer Diagram 212. White cannot castle Kingside until the Bishop on f1 is moved.

106. False. In Pawn magic, the Queening Pawn can change into any piece except a King.

107. True. A Pawn Queens when it reaches the last rank on the side of the chessboard opposite where it started.

108. False. You can make a new Queen even if you still have your original one.

109. False. A Pawn may be promoted to a Rook, Bishop, or Knight, too.

110. True. Promoted pieces and original pieces are identical.

111. False. You can capture an enemy piece on the back rank and promote your capturing Pawn at the same time.

112. False. A promoted Queen, like a natural Queen, is worth 9 points.

113. True. The Queening Pawn is allowed to checkmate the enemy King. Also a different checkmate could occur if the advancing Pawn clears a line for another piece to give a discovered mate.

114. False. A Pawn must reach the 8th rank before promoting.

115. False. Sometimes it is better to make a new Knight, Bishop, or Rook.

116. Pawns may Queen and Kings may CASTLE.

117. A King can never Castle into CHECK.

118. A King can never Castle out of CHECK.

119. The only time a King can move more than one square on a turn is when it CASTLES.

120. The only time a Rook can jump over another piece is when the King CASTLES.

121. When it castles, the King moves two squares toward the Rook.

122. A King can castle Kingside or QUEENSIDE.

123. You cannot castle if the King has been MOVED before.

124. You cannot castle if the Rook has been MOVED before.

Answer Diagram 212

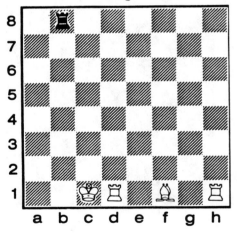

Answers for Chapter 7

1. Yes, Black is stalemated.
2. No, Black is not stalemated. The h-Pawn can move to h6 or h5. Move it to h6 and it's checkmate to White! See Answer Diagram 214.
3. Yes, Black is stalemated.
4. No, Black is not stalemated. The Black King has no move, but the Bishop does. It can move to b5 checkmating White! See Answer Diagram 216.
5. Yes, Black is stalemated. Neither the King nor any Black men can move.
6. The two Kings cannot get any closer to each other. The closest they can get is one square apart.

Answer Diagram 214

Answer Diagram 216

7. A King can never move into check.

8. A King can never move more than one square at a time, except when it castles. When castling, a King must move two squares toward the castling Rook.

9. One King can never checkmate another. A King can protect a piece that gives checkmate, but it can never checkmate by itself.

10. White cannot force checkmate. A checkmate cannot be set up even with Black's help.

11. Black cannot win. A King by itself can never give check or checkmate.

12. The game is drawn. Neither side can win.

13. White cannot win. He has only a King.

14. Black cannot force checkmate. A checkmate cannot even be set up with White's help. In order to checkmate by force, the winning side needs at least an extra Rook. One Knight or one Bishop is not enough.

15. The game is drawn. Neither side can win.

16. White cannot checkmate Black unless Black plays bad moves on purpose. If Black plays bad moves on purpose, White could checkmate in a corner, as shown in Answer Diagram 225, but this would not happen in a real game.

17. Black cannot checkmate White, unless White makes certain very bad mistakes. If White makes big mistakes in just the right ways, Black may win accidentally.

18. The game is drawn. Neither side can force mate.

19. White cannot checkmate. A King by itself has no power.

20. Black cannot checkmate with two

Knights unless a winning position is already set up, as in Answer Diagrams 226–1 and 226–2. White would have to play right into Black's hands to lose. In most cases, one move before checkmate, Black would stalemate White. Try this as an exercise with friends. (See Diagrams 228 to 230.)

21. The game is drawn.

22. White can checkmate. It's tough, but White can do it all the time. The trick is to drive the Black King toward a corner the same color as the Bishop, as shown in Answer Diagram 227.

23. Black cannot win.

24. The game is not a draw. White has a forced win, but he has only 50 moves to do it, as will soon be explained.

25. White's King is on g1 and White's Queen is on b1.

26. Black's King is on g8.

27. This is the first time this position has occurred to our knowledge.

28. White has played Queen on b1 to g6, check. This is written: 1. Qb1–g6+.

29. This is the first time this position has occurred.

30. Black has played King on g8 to h8. This is written: 1. . . . Kg8–h8. (Note that when you're writing one player's move, three dots precede Black's moves, while no dots come before a White move, except the one after the number of the move.)

31. This position has occurred once.

32. White has played Queen on g6 to h6, check. This is written: 2. Qg6–h6+.

33. This position has occurred once.

34. Black has played King on h8 to g8. This is written: 2. . . . Kh8–g8.

35. This position has occurred once. It is

the second time Black's King is on g8. The last time, White's Queen was not on h6, though, so the position is different.

36. White has played Queen on h6 to g6, check. This is written: 3. Qh6–g6+.

37. This is the second time this position has occurred. The first time was after White's first move.

38. Black has played King on g8 to f8. This is written: 3. . . . Kg8–f8.

39. This position has occurred once.

40. White has played Queen on g6 to f6, check. This is written: 4. Qg6–f6+.

41. This position has occurred once.

42. Black cannot claim a draw.

43. White cannot claim a draw.

44. Black has played King on f8 to g8. This is written: 4. . . . Kf8–g8.

45. This position has occurred once.

46. Black cannot claim a draw.

47. White *can* claim a draw.
   If White wants to draw, White must

Answer Diagram 225

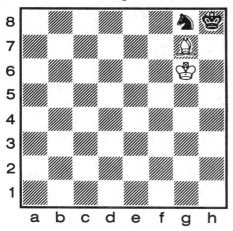

Answer Diagram 226–2

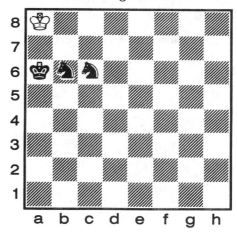

Answer Diagram 226–1

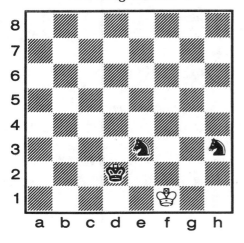

Answer Diagram 227

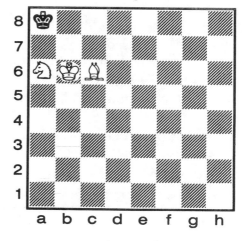

announce that the same position is going to occur for the third time when the White Queen is moved to g6.

You must announce your plans to claim the threefold repetition draw. If you play the move without stating your drawing plans, you lose the right to claim the draw.

Black is losing and would like to claim a draw, but it is White who has the ability to repeat the position and claim a draw, not Black. Black will have to wait for another chance.

48. White has played Queen on f6 to g6, check. This is written: 5. Qf6–g6+.

49. This position has occurred three times.

50. Black cannot claim a draw. No matter what Black now plays, the next position will have occurred only twice.

51. White cannot claim a draw on Black's turn. If White wanted to claim a draw, White should have done so a move earlier.

52. Black has played King on g8 to h8. This is written: 5. . . . Kg8–h8.

53. This position has occurred twice.

54. Black cannot claim a draw on White's move.

55. White cannot claim a draw. No matter what move is played, the position won't be repeated for the third time.

56. The only three-time repetition occurred in Diagrams 233, 237, and 241.

57. White has played Queen on g6 to h6, check. This is written: 6. Qg6–h6+.

58. This position has occurred twice.

59. Black cannot claim a draw. Black must

play his King to g8. It's only the second time this position has occurred.

60. White cannot claim a draw. It's not White's turn.

61. Black played King on h8 to g8. This is written: 6. . . . Kh8–g8.

62. This position has occurred twice.

63. Black cannot claim a draw. It's not Black's move.

64. White could claim a draw if Queen to g6 is played on the next move. That would repeat a position for the third time. But White is ahead by a Queen and doesn't want to claim a draw.

65. White played Queen on h6 to g6, check. This is written: 7. Qh6–g6+

66. This position has occurred four times.

67. Black can claim a draw. If Black wants to play King on g8 to h8, Black should announce the plans to do so and claim a draw. Since Black is behind by a Queen, this is what Black does.

68. White cannot claim a draw because it is not White's turn. Also, White doesn't want a draw, having an extra Queen.

69. The position of Diagram 246 occurred in Diagrams 234 and 242.

70. In chess, you can win a game, you can lose a game, and you can DRAW a game.

71. When you draw a chess game, no one WINS and no one LOSES.

72. A stalemate is a DRAW.

73. It is stalemate when the King has no LEGAL moves to make and neither do any of the King's men.

74. It is a draw if both PLAYERS say it is a draw.

Hidden Checkmates

Are you ready to tackle the checkmate puzzles hidden in some of the diagrams? I hope you know all the things in the seven chapters of *Square One,* because you will need them to solve the puzzles in this section.

There are several kinds of checkmates here. There are mates in one move, mates in two moves, and mates in three moves. These mates are listed by color, depending on who goes first and forces mate.

Under the heading "White Checkmates in One Move," for example, the first number we see is 97a. This means that in the position seen in Answer Diagram 97, White can play and mate Black in one move.

Under the heading "Black Checkmates in Two Moves," you will find diagram numbers for positions that hide two-move checkmates for Black. In these, Black goes first, White replies, and then Black mates.

For those positions listed under "White Checkmates in Three Moves," White goes first, then Black, then White again, then Black again, and finally White mates.

I recommend you begin with the mates in one and then try the mates in two before getting to the mates in three.

The answers to all the checkmate puzzles can be found listed by their diagram numbers in the Checkmate Answers section. For example, in this section under the heading "White Checkmates in One Move," you will find:

97a) 1. Bg1–b6 mate

If you have read the sections of *Square One* that teach chess notation, you know this means White checkmates Black by playing the Bishop from g1 to b6.

The 97a means the checkmate is hidden in Answer Diagram 97. If the checkmate were hidden in Diagram 97, the "a" would not appear, and it would be written as 97.

In the Checkmate Answers section under the heading "Black Checkmates in One Move," you will find:

> 98a) 1. . . . Rc8–c1 mate

If you know your chess notation, you know this means Black checkmates White by playing the Rook from c8 to c1, in Answer Diagram 98.

Note the difference between White and Black checkmates. When White mates in one move, we see the Diagram or Answer Diagram number listed first. When the moves are given, we see the number of the first move listed like this: 1.

When Black mates in one move, the Diagram or Answer Diagram number is also given. Then the number of the move is seen, followed by three extra periods, like this: 1. . . .

The three extra periods are used in both descriptive and algebraic chess notations and mean that White's move, which is always listed on the left, has been left out.

Under the heading "Black Checkmates in Two Moves," you will see:

> 101a) 1. . . .   g4–g3+
>   2. Kh2–h3   Re1–h1 mate

This means that in Answer Diagram 101, Black mates by first moving the g-pawn from g4 to g3, giving check. The White King moves from h2 to h3 to get out of check. Then Black mates with the Rook, moving it from e1 to h1.

A diagram may be listed as a mate for both White and Black, because a number of diagrams in *Square One* hide mates for both sides. As in real games, winning may depend just on whose turn it is. When both sides have mates, if it's White turn, White mates, but if it's Black turn, Black mates.

Some checkmate puzzles have more than one correct solution. In these, you solve the puzzle by finding any of the answers given, but you can give yourself extra points for every additional correct answer you find.

If you want to measure your success on the mates, award yourself 1 point for each correct one-move mate you find, 2 points for each correct two-move mate, and 3 points for each correct three-move mate.

For puzzles with more than one correct solution, give yourself full credit for each extra correct solution you find. Check your results in the Success Table below.

Good luck!

Note to the reader: In order to read the answers completely, you must learn the notational symbols for castling and promotion.

Whether you have White or Black, if you castle on the Kingside it is written **0–0**. If you castle on the Queenside, it is written **0–0–0**.

When you promote a pawn into a new piece, you use a parenthesis ( ) to indicate the new piece. For example, **a7–a8(Q)** means "a7 moves to a8 and becomes a Queen."

Success Table

Category	Points
Junior Expert	(108–138)
Junior Player	(75–107)
Junior Novice	(35–74)
Junior Beginner	(0–34)

WHITE CHECKMATES IN ONE MOVE

97a	113a	148	181a–2	213
104a	114a–1	149	182	214
105a	115a–1	150	184	215
106a	116a	151	188	216
107a	130a	152	189	217
108a	131a	153	190	
109a	144	164	191	
110a	145	172	192	
111a	146	174a	204	
112a	147	179	205	

WHITE CHECKMATES IN TWO MOVES

119	128
120	132a
121	170
123	171
124	181
125	183
126	203
127	207

BLACK CHECKMATES IN ONE MOVE

98a	109a	157	192
99a	110a	158	204
100a	111a	159	205
101	112a	161	214
102a	113a	164	216
105a	114a–1	181	
106a	137a	182	
107a	141	185	
108a	155	188	
	156	190	

BLACK CHECKMATES IN TWO MOVES

101a	118a
103a	163
116a	189

WHITE CHECKMATES IN THREE MOVES

117a	129a
122	160

BLACK CHECKMATES IN THREE MOVES

117a

Checkmate Answers

WHITE CHECKMATES IN ONE MOVE

97a)	1.	Bg1–h6 mate
104a)	1.	Rh5 × h7 mate
105a)	1.	Rd1–d8 mate
106a)	1.	Bh4–f6 mate
107a)	1.	Qh5–f7 mate
108a)	1.	f5–f6 mate
109a)	1.	Qf7–a7 mate
110a)	1.	b2–b4 mate
111a)	1.	b5–b6 mate
112a)	1.	Qa5 × f5 mate
113a)	1.	Qb2–g7 mate
114a–1)	1.	Qh4–e4 mate
115a–1)	1.	Qb2–g7 mate
116a)	1.	Qe6 × e7 mate
130a)	1.	Qh5–e8 mate
131a)	1.	Ba1–e5 mate
144)	1.	Rc1–c8 mate
145)	1.	Qd3–h7 mate
146)	1.	Nh6–f7 mate
147)	1.	Qa1–g7 mate
148)	1.	h6–h7 mate
149)	1.	Bb1–a2 mate
150)	1.	Rg1–g8 mate
151)	1.	Qh1–a8 mate
152)	1.	Ra7–g7 mate
153)	1.	Bg2 × b7 mate
164)	1.	Ba7–b8 mate
172)	1.	Rh8–f8 mate
174a)	1.	Rh1–h7 mate
179)	1.	c7–c8(Q) mate
		or
	1.	c7–c8(R) mate
181a–2)	1.	Qa8–h1 mate
182)	1.	f7–f8(N) mate
184)	1.	c7 × b8(Q) mate
		or
	1.	c7 × b8(B) mate
		or
	1.	c7–c8(N) mate
188)	1.	Qd4–d8 mate
189)	1.	Bg5–d8 mate

190)	1.	Rc7–c8 mate
191)	1.	Qe2–e8 mate
192)	1.	Ne5–f7 mate
204)	1.	Rh1–f1 mate
		or
	1.	O–O mate
205)	1.	O–O–O mate
213)	1.	Qc7–c8 mate
214)	1.	Bf4–e5 mate
215)	1.	Ra7–a8 mate
216)	1.	b6–b7 mate
217)	1.	g3–g4 mate

BLACK CHECKMATES IN ONE MOVE

98a)	1. . . .	Rc8–c1 mate
99a)	1. . . .	Rf8–f1 mate
100a)	1. . . .	Qa4–d1 mate
101)	1. . . .	Ra1–b1 mate
102a)	1. . . .	Nf5–g3 mate
105a)	1. . . .	Qb2–a3 mate
106a)	1. . . .	Rb8–b2 mate
		or
	1. . . .	Na4–c3 mate
107a)	1. . . .	Qd8–a5 mate
108a)	1. . . .	Qd5–h1 mate
109a)	1. . . .	Rd1 × c1 mate
110a)	1. . . .	b7–b6 mate
111a)	1. . . .	Rc8–c1 mate
112a)	1. . . .	Qh4–h2 mate
113a)	1. . . .	Qc8–h3 mate
137a)	1. . . .	Qc7 × h2 mate
141)	1. . . .	Qd8–d1 mate
155)	1. . . .	Bc8–h3 mate
156)	1. . . .	Nf2–g4 mate
157)	1. . . .	Re8–e1 mate
158)	1. . . .	Qc7–h2 mate
159)	1. . . .	f3–f2 mate
161)	1. . . .	Qf5–g4 mate
		or
	1. . . .	Qf5–h5 mate
		or

	1. . . .	Qf5–f6 mate
164)	1. . . .	Qh3–g2 mate
		or
	1. . . .	Re3–e1 mate
		or
	1. . . .	f3–f2 mate
181)	1. . . .	Qa3 × a2 mate
182)	1. . . .	Qd4–d1 mate
185)	1. . . .	f2–f1(Q) mate
188)	1. . . .	e2–e1(Q) mate
190)	1. . . .	g2–g1(N) mate
192)	1. . . .	Qh4 × h2 mate
204)	1. . . .	Qb5 × e2 mate
205)	1. . . .	Qc5 × g1 mate
214)	1. . . .	h7–h6 mate
216)	1. . . .	Ba4–b5 mate

WHITE CHECKMATES IN TWO MOVES

		White	*Black*
119)	1.	Rd1–g1+	Kg8–h8
	2.	Bh4 × f6 mate	
120)	1.	e6–e7+	Kg8–h8
	2.	Nh4–g6 mate	
121)	1.	Qh1–h5+	Nf6 × h5
	2.	Rf2 × f8 mate	
123)	1.	Rf2 × f7	Kh8–g8
	2.	Rf7–f8 mate	
124)	1.	g6–g7+	Kf8 × g7
	2.	Qh3–h6 mate	
		or	
	1.	g6–g7+	Kf8–e8
	2.	Qh3–c8 mate	
125)	1.	Rf1–e1+	Ke8–f8
	2.	Qb2–h8 mate	
		or	
	1.	Rf1–e1+	Ke8–d8
	2.	Qb2–b8 mate	
126)	1.	Ne5–g6+	h7 × g6
	2.	Rf1–h1 mate	
127)	1.	Bc1–h6	Kg8–h8
	2.	Rf1–f8 mate	
128)	1.	Qe2–g4+	Kg8–f7
	2.	Qg4–g6 mate	
		or	

	1.	Qe2–g4+	Kg8–h7
			(or Kg8–h8)
	2.	Qg4–g7 mate	
132a)	1.	Rh1–h8+	Rf7–f8
	2.	Rf1 × f8 mate	
		or	
	1.	Rh1–h8+	Rf7–f8
	2.	Rh8 × f8 mate	
170)	1.	Re6–a6+	Ka8–b7
	2.	Bh3–c8 mate	
171)	1.	Ra8–a7+	any King move
	2.	Rb6–b8 mate	
181)	1.	a7–a8(Q)+	Bb4–f8
	2.	Qa8–h1 mate	
183)	1.	c7–c8(R)	Ka7–a6
	2.	Rc8–a8 mate	
203)	1.	O–O	Kg3–h3
	2.	Rf1–f3 mate	
207)	1.	c2–c3+	Bb7–e4
	2.	O–O mate	
		or	
	1.	c2–c3+	Bb7–e4
	2.	Rh1–f1 mate	

BLACK CHECKMATES IN TWO MOVES

101a)   Black can play many different first moves to mate in two:
Black's Queen could move to a5, a6, a7, a8, or d1.
       or
Black's Knight could move to a6, c6, d5, or c2.
       or
Black's Bishop could move to a6, b5, d3, e2, f1, d5, e6, f7, or g8.
       or
Black's King could move to d1, d3, e1, e2, or e3.
White then must move his King to b2, and Black then mates by promoting the a-pawn, a2–a1, making a new Queen.
Two other mates in two are:

1. . . .	Nb4–c2+

	2.	Ka1–b2	Qa4–a3 mate (or Black could move the Queen to b3, b4, or b5) or
	1. ...		Qa4–d1+
	2.	Ka1–b2	Qd1–c1 mate
103a)	1. ...		g4–g3+
	2.	Kh2–h3	Re1–h1 mate
116a)	1. ...		Qb8–f4+
	2.	Kf2–e1	Rc8–c1 mate or
	1. ...		Qb8–f4+
	2.	Kf2–g1	Rc8–c1 mate
118a)	1. ...		Rh8–g8+
	2.	Kg1–h1	Qa8 × f3 mate
163)	1. ...		Qb3–a2
	2.	Kc1–d1	Qa2–d2 mate or
	1. ...		Qb3–a2
	2.	Kc1–d1	Qa2–b1 mate
189)	1. ...		e2–e1(Q)+
	2.	Kh1–g2	Bh7–e4 mate

	2.	Rf1–a1+	Qd7–a4
	3.	Ra1 × a4 mate	
122)	1.	Nf5–d6+	any King move
	2.	Re5–a5+	b6 × a5
	3.	Rh5 × a5 mate	
129a)	1.	Ne4–f6+	g7 × f6
		(if 1. ... Kg8–h8, then 2. Rb8 × f8 is mate	
	2.	Rb1–g1+	Kg8–h8
	3.	Rb8 × f8 mate	
160)	1.	Be6–f5	Kh8–g8
	2.	Bf5–g6	Kg8–f8
	3.	Qa7–f7 mate	
			or
	2. ...		Kg8–h8
	3.	Qa7–h7 mate	
			or
	1.	Qh7–g1	Kh8–h7
	2.	Be6–f7	Kh7–h6
	2.	Qg1–g6 mate	
			or
	2. ...		Kh7–h8
	3.	Qg1–g8 mate	

WHITE CHECKMATES IN THREE MOVES

117a) 1.   Qd1–a6+   Ka7 × a6
(if 1. ... Ka7–b8, then 2. Qa6–b7 is mate)

BLACK CHECKMATES IN THREE MOVES

117a)	1. ...		Qd7–g4+
	2.	Kg2–h1	Qg4 × f3+
	3.	Kh1–g1	Rf8–g8 mate

Glossary

Advantage—If you have an advantage, you are ahead in material or position. If you have the advantage, you have the better game.

Attack—When you can capture an enemy man next move, you are attacking it.

Black—The player with darker colored pieces is usually called Black, even if those pieces are another color. Black moves second at the start of the game.

Blocked—If you are unable to move because an enemy man is in the way, you are blocked.

Blunder—A blunder is a very bad mistake.

Capture—When you take an enemy man off the board, you have captured it.

Castling—Castling is the only time you can move two men on the same turn. When you move the King two squares toward the Rook and bring the Rook to the other side of the King, you are castling.

Center—The center is the middle of the chessboard. It usually means squares e4, d4, d5, and e5.

Check—A check is an attack to the King without the game being over, because the King can be saved. When the King is in check, you must get it out of check before you can make any other move.

Checkmate—When you checkmate the enemy King, the game is over. Checkmate is an attack to the King that can't be stopped. The checkmated King would be captured next move. When the King is checkmated, it cannot be saved.

Chessman—A chessman is any piece or pawn.

Dark Squares—The dark squares of the chessboard can be black or any other dark color. There are 32 dark squares on every chessboard.

Dark-Square Bishop—Both Black and White have a dark-square Bishop. It is the Bishop that moves on dark squares only.

Defender—A defender is a piece or pawn that guards another piece or pawn.

Development—When you develop a chessman, you are moving the piece to a useful square or moving a pawn out of its way. Your development is how you have positioned your pieces.

Diagonal—A diagonal is a slanted row of squares of the same color. A diagonal may contain between two and eight squares.

Discovered Attack—When you make one move that uncovers another friendly man's line of attack on an enemy man, you have a discovered attack. Sometimes both friendly men, the one that moves and the one that is uncovered, threaten to capture the enemy on the next move.

Double Attack—There are three kinds of double attacks. A double attack can be a threat by one man to capture two different enemy men on the same turn. This is also called a fork. Another kind of double attack could be a threat by two friendly men against the same target. Finally, a double attack could be any two threats by one side against the other.

Double Check—A double check is an attack by two men against the enemy King, one of which gives a discovered attack. In a double check, two chessmen of the same color (both the one that moves and the one whose attack is uncovered by that move) check the enemy King.

Doubled Pawns—When there are two pawns of the same color on the same file, you have doubled pawns.

Draw—When neither Black nor White win the game, it is a draw. There are several ways a chess game can end without either side winning or losing. One way for a draw to come about is called STALEMATE.

Endgame—The endgame is the last part of a chess game. In the endgame someone usually wins by making a new Queen and later setting up a checkmate.

Enemy—If you are playing the light-colored pieces, the enemy is playing the dark-colored pieces. If you are playing the dark-colored pieces, the enemy is playing the light ones. In chess, the enemy is your opponent.

En Passant—*En passant* is a special way to capture pawns. (See Chapter 6.)

Exchange Values—The exchange values are the chessmen's point values. A pawn is equal to one point, Knights and Bishops are equal to three points each, a Rook is equal to five, and a Queen is equal to nine. Because the King cannot be exchanged (the game would be over), the King does not have an exchange value.

Fifty-Move Rule—If no pawn has moved or no man has been captured in 50 moves, the game is a draw.

File—A file is a row of eight squares going up and down the board, from top to bottom.

Fork—A fork is a threat by one friendly man to capture two enemy men.

Half-Open File—A half-open file is a file that has Pawns of only one color on it.

Illegal Move—An illegal move is a move that is against the rules. It cannot be played.

Kingside—The Kingside is the half of the chessboard with the e-, f-, g-, and h-files.

Legal Move—A legal move is a move that the rules allow. It can be played.

Light Squares—The light-colored squares of the chessboard can be white or any other color. There are 32 light squares on every chessboard. Both players must have a light square in the chessboard's right-hand corner at the start of the game.

Light-Square Bishop—Both Black and White have a light-square Bishop. It is the Bishop that moves on light squares only.

Losing the Exchange—When you lose the exchange, you lose a Rook and gain a Bishop or Knight. You gain three points in exchange for five. You lose two points.

Man—A man is a short way to say a chessman. A chessman is a piece or pawn.

Mate—Mate is a shorter way to say checkmate.

Material—Material is a general name for pieces and pawns.

Middlegame—The middlegame is the second part of a chess game, where plans are made and developed.

Notation—Notation is a way to write down chess moves. There are two main kinds, algebraic notation and descriptive notation.

Occupy—When a piece or a pawn is on a particular square, it occupies that square.

Open File—An open file is a file with no pawns on it at all.

Opening—The opening is the first 10 or 15 moves of a game. In the opening, pieces are developed, the players fight for the center, and they castle.

Opponent—Your opponent is the player of the other color. The player trying to beat you is your opponent.

Piece—Knights, Bishops, Rooks, Queens, and Kings are all pieces. Pawns aren't pieces.

Pin—When one piece threatens two enemy men along the same rank, file, or diagonal, it is a pin. In a pin, the less valuable man is between the attacker and the more valuable man. If the less valuable man moves away from the threat, the more valuable piece could then be captured.

Promotion—When a pawn reaches the last rank and changes to either a Queen, Rook, Bishop, or Knight we call it a promotion. Since the Queen is the most valuable piece, usually you make a new Queen.

Protect—When you protect something, you guard it.

Queening—Moving a pawn to the last rank and making a new Queen is called Queening.

Queenside—The half of the board containing the a-, b-, c-, and d-files is the Queenside.

Rank—A row of eight squares going across the board from left to right is a rank.

Removing the Defender—When you get rid of an enemy man's protection by capturing it or threatening it and making it move away, you remove the defender.

Sacrifice—A sacrifice is giving up material for attack or other advantages.

Stalemate—A stalemate is a draw. If the player whose turn it is has no legal move but is not in check then the game is a draw.

Threat—A threat against a chessman means that man could be captured with advantage on the next move.

Threefold Repetition—A threefold repetition is a draw in which the same exact position has occurred at three different times during a game. The player who is going to repeat the position for the third time claims a draw before actually moving.

Touch Move—Touch move is a rule that says the player whose turn it is must move whichever piece or pawn is touched first.

Trade—A trade is an exchange of equal value. In a trade the point value of the men lost is equal to the point value of the men taken.

Underpromotion—When a pawn reaches the last rank and changes into a Rook, Bishop, or Knight, instead of a Queen, it is an underpromotion.

Weakness—A weakness is a square not guarded enough.

White—The player moving the lighter-colored pieces and pawns is called White, even if those pieces are another color. White is the player who goes first.

Winning the Exchange—When you win the exchange, you gain a Rook for a Bishop or Knight. You give up three points in exchange for five. You have gained two points.

Index

About the Author

BRUCE PANDOLFINI is the author of seventeen instructional chess books, including *Chess Target Practice; More Chess Openings: Traps and Zaps 2; Bobby Fischer's Outrageous Chess Moves; Beginning Chess; Pandolfini's Chess Complete; Chessercizes; More Chessercizes; Checkmate; Principles of the New Chess; Pandolfini's Endgame Course; Russian Chess; The ABC's of Chess; Let's Play Chess; Kasparov's Winning Chess Tactics; One-Move Chess by the Champions; Chess Openings: Traps and Zaps;* and *Weapons of Chess.* He is also the editor of the distinguished two-volume anthology, *The Best of Chess Life & Review,* and has produced, with David MacEnulty, two instructional videotapes, *Understanding Chess* and *Opening Principles.*

Bruce was the chief commentator for the New York half of the 1990 Kasparov-Karpov World Chess Championship. In the same year, he was head coach of the United States Team in the World Youth Chess Championships in Wisconsin. Perhaps the most experienced chess teacher in North America, he is co-founder, with Faneuil Adams, of the Manhattan Chess Club School, and is the director of the New York City Schools Program. Bruce's most famous student, six-time National Scholastic Champion Joshua Waitzkin, is the subject of Fred Waitzkin's acclaimed book *Searching for Bobby Fischer* as well as the movie of the same name. Bruce Pandolfini lives in Manhattan.